STORIES FROM INDIA

Jacob Andrews
RESSLER

© 2014 STORIES FROM INDIA
By Jacob Andrews Ressler
Missionary in India from 1899-1908

Published by Mennonite Publishing House, Scottdale PA
Coprighted 1916 Mennonte Publishing House, Scottdale PA

To order additional copies of this book, contact:
Lyle Kropf
336 America Street
Wickenburg, AZ 85390
or call 928-684-5778

 Ridgeway Publishing & Printing Co.
Medina, New York
888.822.7894

to my wife,
whose help and encouragement in my Indian experiences and in the preparation of these stories have enabled me to continue work notwithstanding many hindrances, this little book is affectionately dedicated.

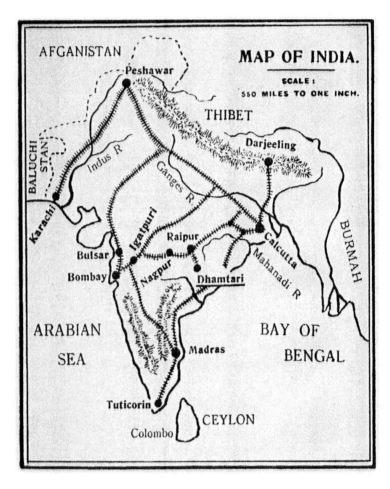

AFGANISTAN

Peshawar

MAP OF INDIA.

SCALE :
550 MILES TO ONE INCH.

THIBET

BALUCHI STAN

Indus R.

Darjeeling

Ganges R.

Karachi

BURMAH

Raipur

Calcutta

Igatpuri

Bulsar

Nagpur

Mahanadi R.

Bombay

Dhamtari

ARABIAN

BAY OF

SEA

Madras

BENGAL

Tuticorin

CEYLON

Colombo

Sketch Map of India, showing Dhamtari and a few other important places.

INTRODUCTION

The stories of this little collection are all from real life and cluster around the experience of the author during his life in India. There have been many changes in the work and life about the scenes of these stories in the past few years, but India changes so slowly that it is fair to suppose that the picture will remain true for some time to come. Other individuals have taken the place of the actors in these stories, but the characters are still the same.

The illustrations are almost all from photographs taken either by the author or by his missionary friends. Special acknowledgments are due to Bro. J. N. Kaufman for the use of a large number of illustrations from his well-chosen collection. A few pictures are also taken from the collection used by Bro. G. J. Lapp on the occasion of his visit to America.

The purpose in presenting this collection to the public is to give as nearly as possible a true idea of some of the experiences of missionaries in India. It is felt that all India needs in order to win the sympathy of true Christians is to be understood. Hence, these stories are true ones, without embellishment or fiction. If people in the home land could but see the work of the Indian missionaries as it really is, could enter into the feelings of those who have laid down so much of what we hold dear on earth that these poor, neglected ones may have a message of salvation presented to them, it would not long be necessary to appeal for help in the form of workers and means, but both would be offered freely.

That God may use this little book to His own glory and that many souls may be led to the light through the instrumentality of the work around which these stories cluster, is the sincere wish and prayer of the author.

INDEX

CHAPTER 1

TWO STORIES TOLD ON A RAINY NIGHT NEAR THE JUNGLE

When the first little house on the compound of the Rudri station had been completed to such an extent that a white man was considered safe in it, I went there to live and to oversee the building work. It was the rainy season of 1902. I had with me the trusted cook and a messenger. On the evening I speak of, the night watchman was there too. I think it must have been the month of August, for the rain was a steady downpour, just like an Indian rain in that month.

The watchman was supposed to see that no one walked off with the poles, bamboos, and tools during the night; but this night was so dark and the rain was so heavy that we had no fear of thieves, and we all sat on the verandah, listening to the rain.

Our thoughts and conversation turned to the subject of tigers. The watchman told his story:

"In the days of Raja Dayaram—I was a boy of ten or twelve then—I went with my father on a pilgrimage to the Juggernaut. There was no

Hindu temples near the bazaar at Dhamtari, India.
The idols are back in the dark recesses under the domes.

railway then, and we went right through the king's country.

"For some time before we passed that way there had been a tiger in the kingdom, and he had gotten very bold. He had killed several of the king's best oxen and many other cattle. Then, becoming bolder, he attacked men and killed a number. Then he no longer was satisfied with cattle, but wanted human flesh as his feed. The whole kingdom was in a state of abject fear.

"At this time a prince, a distant relative of the raja, came forward with a plan to capture the frightful beast. At first, the king would not consent to his plan for a moment. But when man after man was killed and the tiger would not go near cattle and buffaloes, which had been tied up as bait to draw him, at last he consented.

"This was the prince's plan: He offered himself as bait for the tiger. Near a tree, they planted two posts firmly into the ground about fifteen inches apart. The young prince stood between the posts and they tied his feet and legs and his arms tightly to the posts with his hands up over his head. On the tree above the prince sat the shikari, the Native hunter, with his trusty gun.

"The plan succeeded. The tiger came, cat-like, creeping nearer and nearer, until he thought he had his prey within his clutches. He opened his mouth to roar in triumph as he rose to spring, when the flash and report of the gun told that there had been other eyes open too as the tiger had been advancing. The tiger sprang, but the bullet had entered his mouth, and he fell dead at the prince's feet.

"The raja gave the young prince his daughter in marriage, and a large reward in money, and the grateful people showed him every mark of honor and esteem."

What a picture, imperfect though it is, of Him who gave His life for the people of the world!

Then the cook told a story:

"When I was cook for the District Superintendent of Police, just after the last famine, we were on one of his inspection tours in the jungle villages. We came to a certain village in which there had been great fear on account of a child-eating leopard. It would break into houses by climbing up to the roof and tearing off the grass thatching and carry off children at night. The people were in terror.

"The District Superintendent of Police remained in the village fifteen days watching for that leopard. He tried all sorts of bait that leopards are supposed to like—goats, sheep, calves—but not one of them would he touch. While the officer was watching over a calf tied out in the jungle, the leopard would break into a house and carry off a child. At last, he had to give it up. He had other duties to attend to and he had to move on.

"But after he had gone away from the village, a Native hunter, a shikari, did something which no white man would have done. He took a famine orphan that happened to be staying with some folks in the village, and tied it under a tree near the village at night, and then he watched. The leopard came and just as he was about to spring upon the child, the man shot and killed the leopard at the first shot."

I have often wondered how that child was affected by its terrible experience. And I have wondered whether ever anyone found it who knew the story of Him who took the lambs in his bosom and tenderly cared for them, and told it of the joy He can give.

CHAPTER 2

FINDING A LOCATION FOR THE MISSION

When the missionaries of the American Mennonite Mission at the present time are on their way to India, they can answer questions with some degree of confidence.

"Where are you going?"

"To India."

"To what part of India?"

"To the Central Provinces."

"What place?"

"Dhamtari."

"What is to be your work?"

"We are going as missionaries in the American Mennonite Mission."

But when the first missionaries were sailing toward India in the spring of 1899, there was nothing definite to say in answer to any question except the first. We are going to India—we knew that much—but as to where we should locate or what should be our work, all was a mere guess.

A railway station in India with a train standing on the track.
The carriages have doors at the side and are divided into compartments.

We were showered with advice, wise and otherwise. Oh, how we broke the precepts against envy as we met persons who had been in India for years, who knew the languages of different parts, who had just exactly the information we felt we needed so very much, but who couldn't transfer to us the very thing we really needed most of all—experience guided by the divine Spirit.

We landed at Bombay March 24, 1899 and took up temporary quarters at the Temperance Hotel, kept by Mrs. Briggs, in Lower Colaba. E. S. Hume of the American Marathi Mission met us there and gave us a hearty welcome to India. He also gave us some very sound advice, which was a great help to us. We met other missionaries whose advice was helpful, among them Bro. W. B. Stover of the Church of the Brethren, who at that time was at Bulsar, one hundred twenty-five miles north of Bombay, near the coast of the Arabian Sea. He, with his family and associate missionaries, had established a mission at Bulsar about five years previous to this and, since the Church of the Brethren has so very much in common with Mennonites, we felt that their experience was of great value to us—and so it proved.

A meeting with missionaries from Igatpuri, a low hill station eighty-five miles from Bombay along the line of the Great Indian Peninsular Railway, decided our going to that place as our headquarters for our first hot season.

Our Mission Board had instructed us to locate if possible in the area that had been affected by the famine of 1897, since a considerable amount of money from our people had gone to help the sufferers at that time, and it was thought that an opening might be gained in that region more easily than in some other parts. We had been told to locate not nearer than thirty miles from any other mission, and we had decided to locate on a railway if possible.

We were told by persons of experience that these conditions would be very easily met, for India was certainly a very needy field and there were large areas still untouched by the Gospel effort.

Acting on the first suggestion at hand, we started out to find the field.

At Lalitpur in the district of the same name, where a small portion of the North West Provinces, or United Provinces, as they call them now, extends southward between the states of Central India, was just the place we were looking for—so we were told. There was a small Christian community some miles from this place under the control of a society in Bombay, but the Bombay missionaries would be very glad to turn them over to us as a beginning for our work. There was absolutely no other work worth mentioning in the whole district. Yes, to be sure, there was a small effort being made by a missionary lady in the town of Lalitpur itself, but her influence did not reach beyond her compound, and there was positively no hindrance to our going to Lalitpur, establishing our mission, and rejoicing—so we were told.

We went to Lalitpur.

We visited the town.

We found the "missionary lady" referred to.

But since our informant's latest information there had come two or three assistants to the lady, one of them an ordained man from America. They had a well-established orphanage with industrial work that we, so new to the country, regarded with great respect and deference. After one sight of that work, we had no more thought of establishing ourselves in Lalitpur.

But at Lalitpur, we heard of Banda, about halfway between Lalitpur and Allahabad. At Banda the Lalitpur missionaries had once lived. They owned a good bungalow there, which they would willingly sell or rent on easy terms. They were going to concentrate their efforts in the Lalitpur District and would be glad to have their work in Banda taken up by others.

Was there any other work in Banda?

N-n-no; at least none that we need regard. To be sure, the Church of England was there, but they did practically no mission work. Their work is all for and among the officials—so we were told.

We went to Banda.

*A typical scene in an Indian country bazaar. The woman has charge
of a "shop" in which are earthen vessels of all kinds for sale.*

At Banda, we saw and heard many interesting things.

We called on the Collector of the district, an influential official, and he gave us valuable information and advised us to see the missionary at Allahabad who had charge of a sub-station at Banda—a Methodist missionary! And we found, too, that the Church of England had native workers very busily engaged in Gospel work in the city and district of Banda. Two flourishing missions formed the "entirely negligible" work at Banda—and we went on to Allahabad!

We saw the Methodist missionary at Allahabad and he treated us most cordially. He would be glad to have us go to Banda, for then he would have a place to put up when he went to look after his work at that place. We explained our reasons for declining his kind suggestion and he had another suggestion.

At Katni, a railway junction point on the way from Allahabad to Jabalpur, he had a small work to look after, but the native dialect at that place was peculiar and there were not many who spoke this dialect. He would be willing to give this work at Katni over to us entirely and withdraw.

Was there any other work being done?

Oh, no; at least none that we need regard seriously. He believed there was a Church of England man that came occasionally to visit the place but we need pay no attention to him or his work.

And we went to Katni.

Being directed by Natives to the "Missionary's house," we found a large Church of England girls' orphanage and a large place of worship that was regularly visited by a missionary from Jabalpur. A force of colporters and catechists was at work, and there was every evidence that the place was being evangelized far better than we could hope to evangelize it for many years. I afterward met that missionary from Jabalpur and learned to appreciate his kindly Christian spirit.

We returned to Igatpuri without having found what we so much wanted, a permanent location for our new mission.

We examined other information regarding possible locations. We made one trip to Calcutta with this object in view and had the services of W. W. White at our disposal as well as the experience of others less widely known. The information we received was all about on the same basis of quality—it had all to be taken with due allowance.

What was the matter?

In the midst of these experiences, it was very difficult for us to see that there was not a tinge of willful deception in the "information" we had been receiving from so many different "reliable" sources.

But viewed in the perspective of seventeen years we know perfectly that these good people meant to give us the exact truth. They were looking at us and our problems from their own viewpoint and in the light of their own experience. India is so vast and its peoples and conditions are so varied that what is exactly true from one person's attitude is not true at all in another location amid different conditions. In our inexperience, too, we failed to notice the modifications placed by our different informant upon their statements. That which we understood in the way we interpreted their language was not at all what they had in mind as they spoke. Truly India is rightly named "The Land of Contradictions."

The discriminating person never tries to describe "India." He will cautiously tell about some of the customs of some of the people in some of the parts of India. If these modifications are left out another may come and tell of other customs of other people in other parts of India and the two are so vastly different that people would think one or the other or both are drawing too largely upon the imagination for belief.

CHAPTER 3

HOW DHAMTARI BECAME HEADQUARTER FOR MISSION

While we were still living at Igatpuri there came to that place for a vacation some missionaries from Raj Nandgaon, a place about forty miles to the north-west of Dhamtari, on the main line of the Bengal-Nagpur Railway. Knowing of our desire to find a location for our mission, these missionaries of the Pentecost Band told us of a place—Dhamtari—which they had planned to occupy, but which they would leave open for us in case we wished to go there, as they had room for expansion in other directions.

When we were returning from our trip to Calcutta, as we passed by Raipur in the early morning, I looked out of the window and saw a two-foot gauge track leading off toward the jungle. I knew that the intended destination of that track was Dhamtari. I had half a mind to get off the train and spend a day with the missionaries of Raipur and talk over the matter of occupying Dhamtari, but I was very tired, Dr. Page was asleep, I had so little information to go on, and so I stuck to the train and went on to Igatpuri.

Hauling bamboos on Indian carts, the oxen have been removed from the carts for rest.

How small a matter may change a whole chain of events is illustrated in that circumstance. From what we learned afterward, we now know that at that time, if I had gone to Raipur the impression I would have gotten would have been very unfavorable to our choosing Dhamtari as a station. No need to tell the details of those circumstances now. Except in the minds of a very few, they belong to the better-forgotten past. But at that time there were two missions in Raipur in such relationship with each other that either one of them would have given us very little encouragement in going to Dhamtari.

But when we got back to Igatpuri, there was news there that set us in motion in haste and with what we supposed was the most humane purpose. South from Raipur one hundred eighty-three miles, at a place called Jagdalpur, was an orphanage, the result of the famine of 1897. It was founded by that noble pioneer missionary Methodist, C. B. Ward. From two men he had left in charge of the work, came an appeal to the Raj Nandgaon missionaries that they come to relieve the distress they were in. There were no funds and the orphans were in momentary danger of going back to heathendom.

The Raj Nandgaon missionaries invited and urged us to go with them to help rescue the orphans from starvation.

And now there were several "ifs" that figured largely.

If we had known more of Indian conditions, we should have first communicated with the founder of the orphanage.

If we had known more about the condition of the roads in the rainy season, we should have feared to start on such a journey—six hundred miles by rail and one hundred eighty-three miles by cart.

And there were several other "ifs."

But we went. Part of the journey is described in another chapter.

Forty-eight miles from Raipur by the solid road, forty miles by the direct line, forty-six miles by the railway that was then partly built, on the road toward Jagdalpur, is the head of the Sub-district of Dhamtari, a town which at that time had about nine thousand people.

Dhamtari had never been occupied by a mission, though missionaries had visited the place in days gone by. It was more than the required thirty miles from the nearest mission station. It was on the outskirts of the famine region of 1897. The two-foot gauge railway was to be widened to two and a half feet and completed. So here were the conditions we had sought. We had a short look at the place and saw the very ground where the Sundarganj station is now and thought of that place as a desirable location.

We went on to Jagdalpur and found that provision had been made for the immediate needs of the orphanage. Our next concern was to get back to civilization as quickly as possible.

When we got to Raipur, there was no thought of moving Dr. Page at once, so we telegraphed for his wife and she came as soon as she could. Then we held a consultation which resulted in a decision regarding which we never had the slightest doubt but that it was the leading of the Holy Spirit. The other ways were closed. As Bro. Stoll, a veteran missionary of Raipur, who gave us practical aid that can never be estimated, once said, "You tell your Board that you had no other way."

We rented a bungalow that we expected to occupy until we could secure a permanent location. If Dhamtari was closed, we would try elsewhere in the same vicinity. Drug, a station of the main line of railway, between Raipur and Raj Nandgaon, was suggested as a possibility. Dr. Page had planned to go to Igatpuri to get the household goods. On the morning he intended to start, he came to my room and called me, telling me he was sick and that I would have to go. That trip to the jungle had done him a permanent injury.

After the goods were in Raipur we began to learn Indian ways rapidly. We hired a cook and employed servants. As the trip to Dhamtari would have to be made a number of times we bought a tonga and pair of oxen. Bro. Stoll accompanied us on the trip when we made the arrangements for land and also Bro. A. D. Wenger, who was at that time on a trip around the world.

In another chapter there is mention made of the patience needed in dealing with official processes in India. It is embarrassing enough when one is located and is simply waiting for something you'd like to have. But to be without a place that you are sure you may occupy for more than a few days and to be waiting until the exceedingly lazy and slow petty officers draw out their weary conclusions is simply exasperating. That was our experience.

But at last we had the arrangements made and we came home with what was in effect a deed for Sundarganj property recorded and in our pocket.

On the morning of November 22, 1899, Bro. A. D. Wenger and the writer came to Dhamtari to live.

It will be seen how little human planning or wisdom had to do with the choosing of Dhamtari as our head station. In fact, it was, from a human point of view, a series of blunders that led to that place. But even the time of our entering the work could not have been better. The famine had begun and the superstitious could not blame it on the coming of the missionaries, and yet it was just the beginning of the famine so that an impetus was given to the work in that first year that could not have been gained in ten ordinary years. We didn't get the orphans at Jagdalpur, but we got what was better, a station at Dhamtari at just the right time.

CHAPTER 4

HOW A FAMINE CAMP WAS ORGANIZED

In 1897 there was an extensive famine in India.

The rains of 1899 were short in both quantity and duration and, following so soon upon the famine of '97; the famine of 1900 was keenly felt by many classes of people who had not been affected by previous times of stress.

The missionaries reached the place now occupied by Sundarganj station early on the morning of November 22, 1899. A short time before this there had been an experimental relief work opened by the government on the side of Dhamtari opposite from the land of the mission. A tank, or reservoir, was dug at the expense of the Government. Men were paid five pice, or two and a half cents, a day for digging ten hours with a pick, women were paid four pice (two cents) for carrying the dirt out from the tank to the bank, and children were paid three pice (one and a half cents) for helping the women. Women and children used baskets for carrying the dirt on their heads. It was thought that

Group of heathen children sitting on a chabutra, or raised platform, found in almost every Indian village. The woman at the rear is evidently trying hard to get away from the camera, but was not quite quick enough.

if people would be willing to work at these wages, it would be good evidence that there was real want and suffering calling for relief from the government.

Applicants for work soon filled the little tank and a larger tank work was opened beside the road leading from Dhamtari to Raipur. The crop was not a complete failure in the vicinity of Dhamtari, but there was scarcity enough so that the farmers did not need to hire help in their harvest and the poor people, who depended on day's work for a living, came crowding into the relief camp.

Rice is the main food of the great majority of the people in the Central Provinces. It was selling at this time at sixteen seers to the rupee or about a cent a pound. It is estimated that a laboring man should eat about one and a half pounds of rice a day, so the wages given would allow them to eat nearly or quite the normal amount of food. Clothing is inexpensive and no special provision was required for that. As rice advanced in price, higher wages were paid later on.

When we had been a few days in Dhamtari, and were still living in our roofless enclosure in the mango grove, and taking our meals at the dak bungalow, or government rest house, Capt. McNabb, the Deputy Commissioner, came on a visit of inspection to Dhamtari. He met Bro. A. D. Wenger and the writer as we were going to breakfast one morning and asked us about our affairs and plans. He told about the difficulties of government officers in finding work for those who came for famine relief and asked whether we missionaries could not find work for a hundred or two of coolies for a few days until a larger work should be opened. He said the government would furnish the money, and all we had to do was to furnish the people with work and see that they got the money.

Under such circumstances we thought we could furnish work!

The first day a number of men and women came and began digging a ditch around the land of the mission. That ditch was later used as the foundation for the wall that surrounds the compound now. Next day 201 famine workers were on our rolls. After the ditch was dug, we had them do other work. They brought in sand for building from the riverbed, they molded and burned brick, they carried stones from the quarry, and everything that unskilled labor could do was done at the expense of the government. In addition to the work on the buildings, the famine workers dug a number of wells, dug several tanks, built a road out about four miles into the country, and did other work of general and public benefit.

But, instead of having them for a few days, we had those government famine workers for eight and a half months. And, instead of a hundred or two, we had at one time nine thousand on our relief works.

Besides the general relief camp, Dr. Page had the oversight and management of a kitchen in which cooked food was given to children and others unable to work. In this kitchen at one time there were over two thousand fed twice a day. He also had a hospital in which there were at one time one hundred twenty patients. He also had a poor house for homeless persons in which there were as high as eight hundred persons. When the rains came on, the government opened kitchens in the villages, since it was not possible to continue the ordinary relief work in the rainy season. Thinking that Dr. Page could continue his work indefinitely, I consented to look after the relief work in thirty-eight villages in the vicinity of Dhamtari. When the doctor had to leave India shortly after the rains began on account of his health, I was left to look after his work alone until the arrival of Brother and Sister Burkhard in October.

Of course there was much work left undone. We had a Native doctor for quite a while, but he attended only to the hospital and dispensary and I had to keep a pretty close watch even on those institutions.

How could all this be done? One word answers the question: Organization.

In the office there was a young man named Elisha, whom we met in Raipur when we lived there. He could count a little in English and could write a splendid hand in Hindi. He knew my way of saying things in broken Hindi, and he and I could understand each other. As time went on we got nearer together in language and he could act as my interpreter. He could keep a cash account and he had charge of all the registers of the workers. He was responsible for all the cash given out to the relief people.

Under him were gang clerks. Each of the gang clerks had charge of from six to ten gangs, according to the kind of work that was being done. They kept a register of the number of workers in each gang and reported each day to the chief clerk, Elisha. The gangs each had a "mate" who directed the work of the men and women under him.

The normal gang engaged in tank digging had six men with picks, twelve women with baskets, six children with baskets, and one mate with a staff—the sign of his authority. Besides this, each separate work, such as a tank or road or well, had its overseer, who directed the gang mates in their work.

I've often thought of that organization since then when we were thinking about Sunday School work. If I saw a man digging at the wrong place, I would say nothing to that man, but would call the overseer and ask him why that man was working there. He in turn would say nothing to the man, but would call the gang clerk and ask him for an explanation. The gang clerk would perhaps pass the question on to the gang mate and the responsibility would thus be traced down. The advantages of this system can be clearly seen. If I had undertaken to direct the work of the nine thousand—what a muddle it would have been. If I had undertaken to give orders when there were others there to give the orders, the other officers would have lost control of their men. But each man in his place, doing as he was told and obeying orders from the one next higher, made an organization that counted for efficiency. In that way twenty thousand men can be as easily counted as ten.

I wish the army of King Emmanuel might be as faithful always as those famine workers generally were. I wish that in our work for the

Master we might all learn the lesson that each has his place to fill and his own particular duty to perform, and that faithfulness to that duty is what counts and makes the whole a success.

Houses built by Christians in the Sundarganj mango orchard.
The shade proved too dense for health
and these houses have since been abandoned.

CHAPTER 5

INSPECTING A FAMINE KITCHEN

If the only kitchens you have seen are such as are found in American homes, you will have to revise your definition in order to understand what is meant by a "famine kitchen."

In order to get to the point we'll have to go back a bit in the story. When the officials realized that famine was coming in the latter part of 1899, they opened "test works," in various places in order to see the extent of the need. A favorite form of these "test works" was earthwork in the way of tank digging—reservoir building we should say. Tanks would be useful later for irrigation.

The wages offered in these works was supposed to be just barely enough to supply food for the workers and no more. It was reasoned that none would come to work under these conditions except those in actual want.

The way the people crowded into those test works alarmed the officials. Even at the small wage of five pice a day for men, four pice

This is a group of Hindus at worship. The priest sits to our left reading from a Hindu sacred book. The sacred pulsi plant is in front. The man of the house, for whose benefit the "worship" is being conducted, sits to the right. The little girl, dressed in the garb of the better class of Hindus, has evidentially wandered on the scene just in time to be taken.

for women, and three pice for children (a pice is worth half a cent), it became a serious problem to find work for the people to do. And where was the money to come from to pay them?

Soon another problem forced itself upon the attention of the government. People who were very evidently in extreme want and clearly unable to work came crowding in for aid. The "work test" could not be used in their case. So a brilliant mind somewhere in the officialdom of the Central Provinces thought of another plan. It is well known that the caste observing Indian despised eating food cooked by one outside his caste. The people would be offered cooked food. If they were really in need they would accept it in spite of caste rules. Orders were issued to "superimpose the cooked food test upon the work test," and the result was even more alarming to the officials than the work test alone. All sorts of folks came asking for cooked food on some pretext or other. You see, it was far easier to get the food ready cooked than to work all day and then have to cook the food themselves in the evening. Caste might go for the time being—they'd see about that later when there was not such a good opportunity to eat all that was necessary without paying for it.

Suffering there surely was, and want and poverty, but it cannot be doubted either that there were some, perhaps many, who accepted relief simply because it was more pleasant that way. The cooked food test "superimposed" on the work test became a by-word among famine officers until all that was needed to provoke a smile was to say "superimposed."

But the double test was consistently adhered to and its consequences bravely met by the government. When the rains came on—the rains of 1900—tank and road building could no longer be carried on, and yet it was felt that there were many who could not support themselves. The "cooked food" arrangement was extended so as to include all who needed and would accept it. There was a "kitchen" in practically every village in the vicinity of Dhamtari. The rice in these kitchens was cooked in large earthen vessels over a fire made in trenches dug in the ground. At a certain hour each day the persons on relief came together at the kitchen and received their dole of rice and peas.

The rice was purchased by government officers and supplied to the persons in charge of the kitchens at the rate of a pound and a half of rice for each working man a day. Women and children received less. As much as possible the ordinary government servants were used in administering relief. The official land measurer, called the patwari, acted as kitchen clerk in many cases. Often the village schoolmaster was impressed into famine service.

It will readily be seen that such a system would throw strong temptation in the way of one whose rule for honesty is simply, Get all you can as long as you don't get caught. The clerk would be tempted to put his family and all his relatives on relief who really did not need it but found it cheaper to bribe the clerk than to buy food. He would be tempted to enter names on his register which had no existence and draw full allowance of rice, storing the balance in his house against the next time of need.

Because of these many temptations and for other reasons it was necessary to have the kitchens regularly inspected by someone in whom the government had some degree of confidence. Thus in the course of famine procedure it became the duty of the writer to inspect some forty-one kitchens in thirty-eight villages in the vicinity of Dhamtari. About fourteen thousand persons were fed at one time in these kitchens. As prospects of a good crop were in evidence toward the close of the rainy season of 1900, the number on relief was gradually reduced. Later many of the kitchens were closed and those in actual need were allowed to go to kitchens that were retained in certain centrally located villages. The public kitchen at Dhamtari was the last to close. It was a task of no small responsibility to determine who should and who should not be allowed to continue on relief toward the close of the famine.

Here is the village of Gokulpur. We are to "inspect" the kitchen this morning and you are permitted to watch. Word has been sent ahead and the village people on relief are all here seated in rows by families. As we approach, they all rise and give a generous "salaam." You think that you can return the salutation by one nice big "salaam" that is to include them all. But no, the village owner's representative is here, and he gives a separate salaam and you must salaam him in return. Then the clerk wants recognition of a similar nature; and then some of the principal farmers, and they'd all be glad for an individual salaam if your time and patience permitted it. Business is business, and politeness must yield to the stress of the circumstances.

"Bring your register."

"Ji, han, Huzur." (Sir, yes, Your Honor.)

"Namwar, haziri lao." (Call the roll by names).

"Ji, han." (In a very loud voice) "Gobind Rao, Koshta!"

Gobind Rao, the Koshta (weaver) answers timidly, "Hazir," and we go to inspect his family. Wife, three children, aged about (no one knows exactly) twelve, ten, and seven, all on relief. They have a well-fed and well-cared for look.

"Gobind, have you been able to sell cloth lately?"

"A little; I'm a poor man and have children."

"Where do you sell your cloth?"

"In the bazaars."

"Have you any fields in this village?"

"Yes; I have some—not much land."

"Have you sown your fields?"

"Yes; that I have—some."

"How is your rice?"

"Nothing at all—I'm a poor man—I am a man with children."

"Makaddam, how is Gobind's crop?"

"Most excellent, Your Honor."

"Has he weeded his rice?"

"Yes; it is in fine condition."

"Clerk, you'd better take Gobind's name off the register. He is feeding us deceit in hopes of remaining on relief a while longer."

"Very well, Your Honor."

So the list is gone through.

Then the stock of rice is examined and measured. An account has been kept of rice received and used, after the manner of a common cash account, and the amount of rice in stock must correspond to this. General conditions in the village are inquired into and a report is made accordingly to the Deputy Commissioner, the head of the district.

All this is very material and of the earth, earthy.

But while the Indians have their material bodies is the time when we must work with them in order to influence them for the Master. Work of this kind was preliminary to schools and village Bible work that are now returning results in conversions from the ways of heathenism to the way of the true and living God.

CHAPTER 6

DEATH OF A FAMINE VICTIM

The famine was considered over. There was a good crop of rice in the fields. The rainfall of 1900 was more than twice the average—85 inches in the vicinity of Dhamtari—and there was no longer any reason for the maintenance of famine works and the famine kitchens. But the persons who had felt the famine first were also the last to be relieved by the coming of better times—those afflicted with chronic poverty.

This class of people was naturally drawn toward the centers where relief work was kept up the longest, and this brought hundreds of the extremely poor to the vicinity of Dhamtari. The "relief habit" had become so fixed in the case of many of these people that they would have welcomed a continuous state of famine.

The government officers quite naturally took an opposite view of the case, and required that the extremely poor be provided for according to the custom in normal times, each in his or her own village.

During the rains following the famine, before definite steps had

Rajakahn, the Mohammedan messenger, and a beggar woman at the east gate of the Sundarganj compound. The mango grove beyond is flooded with water and the water is pouring in at the gate. He is in full Indian children's dress. This picture is the author's first attempt at photography, and was taken in the rainy season of 1900.

been taken by the government to get people back to their own villages, a large number of old and infirm people gathered in the neighborhood of the mission. Some of them depended for a living on begging in the town. About fifty to a hundred of them came twice a day to get the passia, or poured off water in which the rice had been cooked for the orphan children. Many people give this passia to their oxen to drink and it has some nutriment in it, but when used as an exclusive diet, it is rather weak. Some of the people who came for it to the mission ate no other food.

Most of the people who came for the rice water went to other places for the night. Some had acquaintances in the town of Dhamtari who allowed them to sleep on their verandahs or near their houses. About a dozen of them remained all the time near our compound, where the eaves of the carpenter shop projected over the wall on the outside. They had no other shelter.

One evening I was out there at the carpenter shop seeing about the work and I happened to look outside the gate. One of those poor people who had been staying outside the wall began to beg to be admitted into our institution and under our care. "Write my name," was the way she put it, for she had seen persons admitted to the hospital, and to the orphanage, and the placing of the name on the register was the important thing to her mind. Would that the name of everyone who reads these lines might be found on the register of the Lamb's book of life!

I rapidly reviewed the situation in my mind. Here was this woman, needy, it was true, but not more needy than the dozen others who were there by her side. If we took her in, we must take in the dozen or be unjust. If we took in the dozen there would be a hundred there the next day. If we took in the hundred there would likely be a thousand there in a week. It was the business of the village owners, not ours, at that time to care for the helpless ones. The abundant crop in the fields would give them ample means to do so. Besides, we were very young as an institution and were busy getting our bearings as a mission.

And thinking of it from another point of view, how could we take her in? She was not a proper subject for the orphanage—she was a woman of thirty-five or more. She was not a patient for the hospital—she was not sick, only hungry. The kitchen and the poor house, that were open a short time before, had been closed by orders of the government. All this I thought of as I rapidly looked the matter over, but all I said was, "What can we do? I can do nothing for you." And I turned away.

Next morning I went back to see about the carpenters' work. One of the men remarked that there was a corpse lying outside the wall. I went and looked and recognized the very woman who had about twelve or fifteen hours before pleaded with me for mercy and I had refused! She had died during the night. As I stood there by that lifeless clay, there came to me what seemed to be a voice, clear as spoken words could have made it: "I promised to supply all your need, and ye would not believe!"

Some time before this we had adopted as the motto of the mission Phil. 4:19: "But my God shall supply all your need according to his riches in glory in Christ Jesus." If the needs of these people were our needs we certainly failed to exercise the trust we should have.

It was about this time that we were getting letters of warning from our friends in America, telling us that we should limit our benevolence, that we should not take in every beggar that happened to come along. We were told that our people in America would not stand by us if we continued to be so tenderhearted. I have often wondered what our good strong brethren would have done had they been in our places at that time in India.

That was one solitary case. There were many other victims to the dread scourge of famine. Cholera came at one time and destroyed many lives. It almost broke up our camp. Our head sweeper was apparently well at noon one day, and by three o'clock in the afternoon he was a corpse—cholera. The kitchen peon died almost as suddenly.

One man came to us early in our famine experience. The kitchen had just been opened. He was told to wait a short time until food could be prepared for him. Before he was asked his name and village, he became unconscious and soon afterward expired—our first case of death from actual starvation. Alas, he was not the last.

Many people have thoughtlessly blamed the British Government for such deaths. The government officials battled nobly with the monster of famine. They made almost superhuman efforts to get food supplies into districts where it was scarce. Often people hoped against hope, and refused gratuitous help until it was too late.

It must be remembered that transportation is a tremendous problem in a land like India, where railways are few and far between. In the rainy season of 1900, the time when the pinch of famine was severest, the Raipur-Dhamtari railway was not finished. The last fourteen miles of the journey had to be made by cart. In the month of August there was one continuous heavy rain for ten days and even the "solid" road from Kurud to Dhamtari, under the heavy cart traffic, became like a swamp. Near where the Dhamtari station now is I saw in a space of fifty yards four loaded carts sunk in the mud to the axle—deserted. The mud was so forbidding that no one dared to venture in either to steal or to save the cargo. Against such odds did British officials labor to supply the people with food and save them from starvation.

The saddest thing about these deaths from starvation was that the people died without a knowledge of the way of salvation. They hungered for natural food, but they had no longing for the bread of life, for they had never heard of the blessed Savior who gives it.

Sad fate.

CHAPTER 7

HOW A MISSION STATION WAS PURCHASED

As the pinch of privation became keen in the famine time, families were often separated. Cases of parents deserting their children were common. Many parents lost their lives from starvation and the diseases which came as the result of famine, such as cholera and dysentery. Famine usually leaves a great train of weakness and suffering even worse than actual hunger.

Early in the famine, children came to the missionaries for help. The mission at Dhamtari never solicited children for their orphanage. They took in all who were felt to be really in need and deserving help. At one time, there were over six hundred children in the orphanage.

As long as the famine kitchen was in operation, the children were fed at the expense of the government and the great problem was to keep them physically in such a condition that they might again recover their normal health and strength, without much thought of preparing them for making their own livelihood. It was soon felt, however, that

Plowing in India. The plow is the same as that used in Bible times in Palestine. It consists of a crooked stick with a tongue attached for applying the "motive power," and a handle for guiding. The point is shod with iron.

the nine acres of land on which the mission buildings stood were not large enough for the work that would have to be carried on in connection with the mission later on. The children would have to be provided for beyond the period of their life in the orphanage.

Just back of the mission compound is the Sunderganj Mango Grove. It contains seventeen acres of land and has over five hundred mango trees growing on it. It belongs to the government, and the fruit had been auctioned off every year to the highest bidder. We thought that if we were to get possession of that grove we might erect buildings on the higher portions of it and thus relieve the congested condition of our compound.

Getting land in India is generally a tedious process.

We sent a letter to the Deputy Commissioner asking whether we could acquire the mango grove and, if so, on what terms. The Deputy Commissioner sent a letter to the Tahsildar (Judge) of Dhamtari asking for particulars. The Tahsildar sent a letter to us asking for our version. We sent a letter to the Tahsildar with our version. The Tahsildar sent our letter with his letter to the Deputy Commissioner at Raipur. The Deputy Commissioner sent the letter of the Tahsildar with his letter to us stating terms. I wrote to the Deputy Commissioner asking for an interview. The Deputy Commissioner granted an interview. That was a little relief to the monotony. I called on the Deputy Commissioner at Raipur. I told him our story. In reply he said that he could not give better terms himself and as an officer of the government it was his duty to get all out of the land that he could; but as a friend he would advise us to appeal from his decision to the Chief Commissioner of the Central Provinces through the Commissioner of the Chhattisgarh Division. I thanked him very much for the suggestion and went home and wrote a letter to the Duputy Commissioner asking him for better terms than he had offered in his previous correspondence. The Deputy Commissioner sent my letter with his to the Commissioner. Now, in the good old days a Commissioner did not bother much about giving decisions but just forwarded the matters onto the Chief Commissioner for decision. But this particular Commissioner was not of that kind. He sent a letter to the Deputy Commissioner asking some questions. The Deputy Commissioner sent the letter of the Commissioner to the Tahsilder of Dhamtari with a request that he get the desired information. The Tahsildar sent the letters of the Commissioner and the Deputy Commissioner to us with request that we furnish the needed statistics. We furnished. The Tahsildar sent the statistics to the Deputy Commissioner and the Deputy Commissioner sent the information to the Commissioner. The Commissioner sent the whole matter to the Chief Commissioner. Then the Chief Commissioner wanted to know something. His fourth Secretary sent a letter to the Commissioner. The letter and copies of the letters came down the stairway through the Commissioner, Deputy Commissioner, Tahsildar, and us. The reply went up the same stairway.

Are you tired of reading?

We were tired of writing.

If missionaries did not have patience they could not be missionaries.

Patience is a good thing for almost everybody —yes, everybody—to have. If the kind reader doesn't have it, just let him begin right now to acquire some. I couldn't tell you how often the correspondence went up and down that official stairway, but at the end of about eighteen months we got a letter containing a lot of copies of letters from officials high up telling us from no less authority than the court of the Viceroy himself that we could have the land on what we considered very good terms.

But while we were patiently waiting we started investigating on another line.

Along the Konker road, out about seven miles from Dhamtari, we had seen a tract of land which we thought would make a good place for a mission home. We tried to buy a portion of the village from the owner, one Apaji, and he was willing to sell, but wanted such an extortionate price that we just declared the deal off and quit.

The mango orchard deal was still pending with government.

A distant relative of Apaji named Nilkanth Rao then offered to sell us land in the village of Rudri. We wanted twenty-five or thirty acres. He was willing to sell us that much or more. We found out that he had a debt of two thousand rupees which he wished to cancel and we changed our tactics. We began to dicker for more land instead of less money. It would be too long a story even for this collection of stores to tell all about the different meetings we had with Nilkanth Rao and the different propositions that were made. But our bargaining ended up by an agreement on our party to pay two thousand rupees ($6,666.66) for fifty acres of land when we got the money. We told the owner that we did not have the money and that we did not know when we should have it. We were at that time living on scarce supplies, having barely enough for our daily needs, let alone thinking of buying land. "Never mind," said Nilkanth Rao, "If you get the money in a year from now I'll sell then—or any other time."

Some time before this ten dollars had been given for the girls in the orphanage. We did not know how it should be invested. One morning while we were in prayer one thought came to all of us. When we arose from our knees, we all looked as if we knew what the ten dollars were for and we told each other our thoughts—a new station for the girls' orphanage.

Then a little later a brother in Illinois sent word to Brother Burkhard that he and his wife had decided to give five hundred dollars toward the India mission, and wished to know what feature was most in need.

Brother Burkhard at once replied that we would be glad to have it for the girls' station. At the time we made our margin the five hundred dollars had not arrived. We had been to see the land at Rudri on Friday. On Monday came the mail from America with a letter containing a draft of four hundred dollars from a man who was not a Mennonite but whose parents were Mennonites. He did not know our needs or wants. He requested that the four hundred dollars be used, not for food or clothing, but for some permanent investment for the mission as a memorial to his parents. Could there be any question as to how that money was to be used?

Four hundred dollars would be twelve hundred rupees. Not enough to pay the two thousand we had to have for our purchase, but then those five hundred were still to hear from, so we sent word to Nikanth Rao that we would be ready for business as soon as the land could be measured and the papers made out.

It takes much time in India to make out papers.

Before the papers for the transfer were made out, along came a gift of four hundred dollars from two brethren in Illinois, who had known of the needs of the girls' station, and this money was specified for that use.

Twelve hundred rupees more!

And the deal in regard to the mango orchard was still pending.

When we had paid the two thousand rupees for the fifty acres at Rudri, we still had four hundred and thirty rupees to begin our building work. Then came the five hundred dollars from the other brother and we pushed the building work as fast as we could. After Rudri was securely in our possession, came the answer referred to before in regard to the mango orchard. See how God overruled our plans for our good. If we had gotten that mango orchard as soon as we had asked for it, it is possible that we should have tried to erect the girls' orphanage building on it; and we all know how much better Rudri was for that purpose. We also see how greatly the Sundarganj station needs the orchard for a breathing space. Truly God is good to His children.

We all felt and still feel that Rudri station and the mango orchard came to the American Mennonite Mission in direct answer to our prayer.

Moreover, out of those early negotiations, came the village. For the portion of land we had been trying to buy before we got Rudri, was no other than a portion of the village of Balodgahan.

It would make this story too long to tell about the negotiations for Balodgahan, but it shows how business must be done in a primitive civilization to tell that the money had to be paid in the presence of the court Registar and that not in notes or by check, but by hard cash in silver. The price was eight thousand rupees. It takes about forty rupees to weigh a pound. We had the eight thousand rupees in boxes and they weighed two hundred pounds. We had a couple of coolies to carry the money and a couple of peons to guard it. When the money had been paid over, one of Apaji's creditors got most of it and asked us for the loan of four boxes to carry it back to Dhamtari. We lent them to him.

Whenever our faith began to waver, and the road seemed hard, it always helped to establish us to think of how we got these pieces of land—Rudri, Balodgahan, the Sundarganj Mango Orchard.

CHAPTER 8

PREACHING IN A FOREIGN LANGUAGE

When Peter was in Judea, he could not hide his Galilean origin. The moment he began to talk, the people of Jerusalem thought, if they did not say, "Thou are a Galilean; thy speech betrayeth thee."

Very few persons who remove from one country to another ever learn the language of the land of their adoption so perfectly that they do not betray the land of their birth in their pronunciation or idiom or manner of speech. How readily we recognize the Scotchman or the Irishman or the Londoner, as he gives his first sentence of greeting. He probably thinks he is talking his very best "American," but there is something about the turn of his tongue that gives him away. So the Frenchman and the German may readily be recognized and distinguished one from the other even if we did not see the one we heard speaking.

So, too, when one is traveling to the east side of the Atlantic and hears outside the door one morning a strong, nasal twang, saying "I

Mission school at Igatpuri, India, in charge of American missionaries.
The Brahmin teacher, recognized by his sacred cord, is seen standing
beside the missionaries.

guess this is the place," he cannot help saying, "There is an American, fresh faced from the land of catarrh."

The missionary to India has exactly the same difficulty in the way of language that the Continental European has when he comes to America. In some respects his difficulties are greater, for the dialects of India are so numerous that he can never hope to learn the exact idiom of the people he is to work with, much less their manner of pronunciation.

Of course the missionary takes up one of the standard languages that have been reduced to writing and have a literature of some extent. But if he masters the language of his books, he will find that the great mass of the people speak among themselves a dialect different from the written language and they have difficulty in understanding his speech with all its foreign peculiar mispronunciations. It is very common to have as an answer to your early efforts at speaking the vernacular to an Indian met with a polite, "Sahib, I don't understand English!" (Sahib, Angrezi nahin samjhat hun.)

Such an experience is discouraging enough to one new to the country but to have it occur after a year and a half of life in the land and active service in famine work savored a bit of the exasperating. I was in the office when a man came to the door with some matter that pertained to the work of the Public Works Department. Mr. Smith, whose quarters were by the Dak Bangla, or Government Rest House, was the representative of that department in those those parts, so I said to the man in front of the door, "Smith Sahib ke pas jao, Dak Bangla ke pas." Our American friends would not suspect that of being English for a moment, but the man in front of the door smiled politely, and said the fatal words, "Angrezi nahin samajhta hun."

The trials of the famine had been many, but this was the last straw. "I felt desperate. I suppose I looked for it; for when I said vehemently (in Hindi, of course), "Who's talking English?" the man quickly stood on one foot, joined his hands in front of his face as if in a prayer and said humbly, "Muaff karo, Sahib Ji!" (Forgive me, honorable Sir!) I had only said to him, "Go to Mr. Smith by the Dak Bungalo." I had been preaching (or trying to) for several months. What a revelation that was to me as to the possible amount of my "sermons" that was being understand. How little I knew the workings of the Indian mind. A little later if such a thing had occurred as a man with business with the Public Works Department coming to the small space in front of my door I should have saved several minutes of valuable time by leading a conversation something like this:

"My brother, you have a message for the gentleman of the P.W.D.?"

"It is true, Your Honor."

"There is a Dak Bangla near here, not?"

"Ji, han; each hai." (Sir, yes; true is)

"By the Dak Bangla is a tent; do you understand?"

"Ji, han; ji han."

"In the tent you will find a Sahib (gentleman) saying: understand?"

"Ji, han!

"That gentleman in the tent is the Sahib of the Public Works Department; understand?"

"Ji, han; how could I not understand?"

"Go to him!"

"Ji, han! Salaam, Sahib Ji."

"Salaam, brother!"

Taking the cue from experiences like this, when we go before an audience to give the message of salvation, instead of "taking a text," and preaching a formal discourse, we begin by asking some simple questions regarding things with which we know they are familiar. If they show that they understand your language you will gradually lead up to the subject nearest your heart. But you will frequently pause in your discourse to ask questions by way of testing the capacity of understanding your "Sahib Hindi."

In South India a missionary had spoken he supposed was a sermon of normal length. He supposed, of course, that every word of it had been understood, for he had preached his best in the vernacular of the people. At the close of the sermon, an Indian brother was asked to lead in prayer. In his prayer the Indian brother thanked the Father for having sent so wise and good a missionary among them, but, he prayed, "Teach him quickly to speak our language, for thou knowest that we do not understand English!"

His pronunciation had been so very poor that the Indian brother, even one accustomed to earring missionaries speak, had not understood a word, but thought he had preached in English.

Another missionary, also in South India, preached in the vernacular and had referred to the barren fig tree with leaves. Now it happens that in this particular language of South India the word leaf and the word for rat are nearly alike to the Western ear. There is one of those mysterious turns of the tongue that makes the difference. The missionary got the wrong turn of the tongue. After the sermon, one of the Indian sisters came to an older missionary lady and asked whether it is true that in America the rats grow on trees!

Such an experience is discouraging.

But the missionary true to his name is not easily discouraged. He has had an experience in his contact with Jesus that makes him want to tell his message to the one who has not heard it. This desire will cause him to put forth energy in acquiring a strange language as nothing else will.

The Hindustani language is spoken by nearly one third of the people of India as what they call their "first language." In addition to those who prefer Hindi to any other, there are a great many others who speak Marathi, Gujarati, Bengali, Punjabi, and other language as a "mother tongue," and also understand and speak Hindi. In India, outside the Hindustani speaking area, we have often been asked what is the difference between Hindi and Hindustani. According to one grammarian, Hindi is the general name for a group of languages and dialects. Its two main branches are High Hindi and Urdu, also known as Hindustani. Another grammarian gives the classification I prefer: the general name is Hindustani; there are two main branches of Hindustani, one called Hindi, and the other Urdu. Hindi uses the Sanskrit alphabet and derives its classical vocabulary from the Sanskrit, while the Urdu uses the Persian or Arabic alphabet and derives its classical vocabulary from Persian and Arabic. The words of common life are the same in both branches and the grammar is nearly the same. Both branches have many dialects. The Sanskrit alphabet, which is used in Hindi, is strictly phonetic and is read from left to right. The Urdu is more difficult. It is not entirely phonetic, and is written and read from right to left. Both alphabets have been "Romanized," though the Roman Hindi is little used, since the ordinary Hindi alphabet is so simple and easy to learn.

As an illustration of the difficulties of pronouncing Hindustani try to pronounce the word for seven, "sat,: giving "s" its English sound, "a" the Italian sound as in "far," and for "t" place the tongue on the teeth, but do not give the breathing necessary for saying English "th." Now try the word sixty, "sath." "S" and "a" have the same sounds as in the word seven, For "th" place the tongue back so as to almost touch the soft palate and breathe a distinct "h" sound. Practice these two words until you can pronounce them; then get someone who does not know Hindustani to see whether he can hear the difference between the two. You will appreciate some of the difficulties in making yourself understood in an Indian vernacular. Many pairs of words can be chosen whose meaning is far more divergent than seven and sixty, but whose pronunciation differs only by a breathing or by a turn of the tongue. If the new missionary knew what he actually said as he slightly mispronounced certain words, he would be greatly embarrassed.

For reasons that will be readily seen, it is the aim of the missionary to train Indian worker as soon as possible who can be his instrument in direct dealing with the non-Christians. In order that the Indian worker may be successful he needs to keep in close touch with the missionary. Language is not the only difficulty in the path of the ambassador for Christ. The Indian Christian means to do well. He has been thoroughly converted and the power of Christ is as great in his case as in that of any American or European. But the Indian has had generations and generations of evil habits back of him and the grooves of wrong deeds have been worn into his character deep and wide. He not only knows the minute shades of meaning in the words of the dialect of the people, but he knows their subtle ways of sinning from his infancy. That which is entirely meaningless to a missionary is coming to a cunning and powerful temptation to the Indian worker.

Is it any wonder that the Indian missionary asks for the prayers of the people at home? Between him and the people he would reach is a wall of difference in language, thought, habit, manner of life, taste, prejudice, and custom. Through his Indian assistant he must allow for a mass of evil influence, the existence of which he recognizes, but whose force he is entirely unable to measure.

Who is sufficient for these things?

ईश्वर आत्मा है और

अवश्य है कि उसका

भजन करनेहारे आत्मा

और सच्चाई से भजन

करें ।

CHAPTER 9

BRINGING HOME A SICK MISSIONARY

We were coming home from our memorable trip to the jungles in month of July, 1899. We did not know as much about India as we did afterward or we should never had gone. If we even had felt the imperative necessity for going, a little more knowledge of the country would have enabled us to make better preparation for the journey and so escape some of the dangers we encountered.

There were four white men in the party. Brethren Hotle and Good of the Pentecost Band at Raj Nandgaon, Dr. Page, and the writer. On the return trip we had two Native boys, two cart drivers and a "cook" that did not know how to cook.

Of the four missionaries who were in that party, two are in America now because their own health broke down, one is in American because of his wife's health, and the fourth, having been born in India of English parents, is still in India, but not in mission work. There were no striking events on the return trip until we neared the borders of Konker State at the top of the Bastar range of mountains.

An India cart on tour. One need not wonder that the Indian traveler is not in a hurry. He has all his physical needs with him wherever he goes and anywhere is a soon as home to him.

We were going along peacefully and without thought of anything to disturb us, when suddenly we saw a pea-fowl crossing the road ahead. To a party of travelers who had to depend very largely on the gun as a means of obtaining food, that was rather exciting and the gun was gotten ready more quickly then it takes to tell this. Brother Page took the weapon and soon we had plenty of meat for two whole days. Two hours later Dr. Page was down with fever. He had had it two days before this but did not say anything about it. Toward evening he recovered from the attack and was, apparently, little the worse for it.

Two days after the event of the pea-fowl, he took a chill and subsequent fever that made us realize that we had a sick man on our hands. His temperature went up to 105.75° and he was delirious at times. We had only a rude hut for shelter and we had to watch him all the time.

By a forced march that night we reached Jagtara at about nine o'clock in the morning, and Dhamtari nine miles further on, late in the afternoon. The road from Jagtara to Dhamatri was very rough and Dr. Page suffered much from the jolting of the cart. He was semi-unconscious from the pain a good deal of the time.

You will remember that this was before there was a mission at Dhamtari, and before Dhamtari had been finally selected as the home of the mission. Brother Hotle found letters from home at the Dhamtari post office, and decided to push on to Raj Nandgaon next morning as fast as he could. He was afraid the illness of Dr. Page might delay us indefinitely and he was anxious to be at home. Brother Good could speak Hindi perfectly and it was felt that we should be safe in his hands.

But about an hour after Brother Hotle had departed for home, Brother Good went down with high fever. We had good quarters in the day bungalow, but imagine my predicament with two sick men to wait on, no provisions for their comfort in the way of food-stuffs, and a very meager supply of Hindi by which to make our wants known. While I was giving attention to one of the patients the other would call out for immediate help. In that way they kept me trotting back and forth from one room to the other the greater part of the day. With the kindly aid of the Tahsildar, or Native judge, we secured another cart to help us on home. Brother Good was put into that cart and Brother Page into another. The two Native boys went into the third. The cook had gone on with Brother Hotle. With our new outfit we started toward Raipur and civilization about six o'clock in the evening. I walked along by the side of the road with a lantern as soon as it grew dark. At daybreak I crept into the cart beside Brother Good and slept until we reached the Darba Rest Hut, about an hour later.

That was Brother Good's "off day" for the fever and he was able to do something in the way of arranging for the next night's trip. Dr. Page declared that he could not stand another mile of the rough travel by cart and we had to plan some other way to get him the remaining twenty-three miles to Raipur. Fortunately a Native official came along and helped us to arrange a bed and eight strong men to carry him in.

We started early in the evening. The two carts that had come all the way were sent out about two hours ahead. I had planned to go with the coolies who carried the doctor for a short distance and then fall back and ride in the cart with Brother Good until the moon set, then go out and carry the lantern. After about five miles, we got a considerable distance ahead of the cart and waited. We waited quite a while and still there was no cart. We thought we heard the bells on the oxen in the distance.

With much difficulty I got the men to understand that they should go on slowly while I went back to see about the cart. I went back about a mile and found that the sound we had heard was frogs in a pond. Then I remembered that there was a short cut in the road across the hard plain just at that place and I figured that the cart must have gone by that cut-off. I started on to catch up with the cart and the men carrying Dr. Page.

I've passed that cut-off many a time since and have thought of that night of weariness and adventure, I suppose, every time I see it. It is near the Abhanpur station on the Raipur-Dhamtari railway.

Now, Indian coolies carrying a sick man do not walk slowly. They have sort of easy, swinging trot that is pretty hard for a white man to keep up with. And I had been tired and footsore before I started away from Darba. I couldn't tell you all the things I thought that night as I walked alone, in writing a week. I heard the jackals howl as they crossed my path before me and behind me. I was anxious to get to the others before the moon set so I could guide them by the light of the lantern. Several times I thought I had found them, then it turned out to be other carts, and I was disappointed.

At last, twelve miles by the mile-stones form Darba, I came up with the cart, got the lantern from it, and started out by the wrong road. There was another cut-off there of which I had not known, and if that driver had not seen me I would then and there have lost my way and this story might never have been written. As it turned out afterwards, the fate of the American Mennonite Mission hung on a very slender cord at that moment. But God was watching and directed the sharp eyes of the driver. He called out "Aisa nahin" (Not that way), and directed me on the right road.

A short distance ahead I found the men with the Doctor and lighted the lantern. He had not known about my experience in missing the cart and was anxious to go on. So on we went and I carried the lantern until we arrived at Raipur just as the missionaries were ready to begin their day's tasks.

Brother Good met us at the verandah. He wondered how we would get Dr. Page up to his room. I said I thought that he and I could carry him. When he took hold of him he realized how much he had suffered. One of us could have easily have carried him so far as the weight was concerned. For six days be had not retained any nourishment and had suffered most of the time from high fever accompanied with vomiting and diarrhea. Under the care of the Civil Surgeon, and with the nursing of his wife, our patient rallied promptly, but the efforts of the trip remained with him, and probably shortened his term of service in India.

I had walked nearly the whole of the distance from the jungle to Raipur, one hundred and eighty-three miles. During the last ninety-six hours of the journey I had walked eighty miles and slept rather less than twelve hours. During our halts on the journey, my time had been taken up with watchful waiting on the sick. I was a bit tired. Perhaps the walking had something to do with it!

The hand of God was in that journey to Jagdalpur. As we look back at it, there seems to have been no human reason that could have justified the expedition; but through it the American Mennonite Mission found a home, and the marvelous results of that work amply justify the conclusion that it is a work of which we may truly exclaim, "What hath God wrought!"

CHAPTER 10

NATIVE TREATMENT FOR LUMBAGO

While we were at Igatpuri waiting, Dr. Page was called to see a sick man whose case was of special interest. You know we waited at that interesting hill station while we took our first steps in Hindi and decided by inquiry and investigation where the future of our mission in India should be.

This "case" began in chronic alcoholism. The man was a victim in the drink habit—for in India, as elsewhere in the world, Satan knows that the tempting cup is a faithful means of drawing people firmly into his snares. His kidneys were diseased and his liver was not in good order and he had suffered a long time from diarrhea. He was under the supposed treatment of a Native medical man but the treatment did not seem to do him much good.

He claimed to have stopped drinking strong drink.

Naturally such a complication of physical troubles brought on pain in his back and they called his trouble lumbago. A native "doctor" —not

Group of representative lepers and their attendants. Seated in the center is the
Mohammedan doctor, who had medical charge of the asylum for a long time.
At his right sits Johan, a brilliant Christian, who was caretaker.
He has since gone to his eternal reward.

the medical man already referred to— heard of the patient and claimed that he could cure the man.

An Indian "doctor's" methods are sometimes strenuous. They seem at times to have gained a faint glimpse of the Homeopathic principle of "like cures like." I am not sure that this practitioner had thus reasoned it out, but if he had, he must have reasoned that as the man had pain in his back the way to cure him would be to give him a new dose of pain from some outside source and he'd get well. At any rate he tried it.

He had the man bare his back and he took an iron hammer and pounded the man's back with it. Evidently the blows were not light ones. The dose was too heavy. It produced "the drug effect." The man's back got very, very sore. Great clots of blood could be seen under the skin.

Now what? The "doctor" had another resource. His treatment was going to come out all right, so he said, but here there was a lot of bad blood that had to be gotten rid of. He order them to put on leeches. They got about two dozen of these animals and put them on the poor man's back and they promptly filled up. Now, most of us have an abhorrence for a leech. It lives on sucking human blood. Sometimes they have been used with success for relieving congested parts, but two dozen of them on one victim is putting it rather heavily in one spot. A few days later there was an abscess formed high enough to contain a quart of puss. At this stage of proceedings Dr. Page was called upon the scene. He was horrified sufficiently to call me to go with him and see the awful condition of the man and his surroundings and I wrote a description of the case for publication in America. We predicted the man could not possibly live until the news of the case got to America. It looked as if the abscess was sure to cause death. If it opened internally the poison would kill him, and if it were opened with a lancet externally, he would be liable to die from the shock.

Some of the symptoms of his trouble yielded readily to proper treatment; but that abscess! And his surroundings!

He was in a room not over eight by ten feet in dimensions. The only door opened on the street not over six feet wide. There was no window.

His bed was on the floor and consisted of a couple of blankets and a rude pillow. The only other furniture consisted of a small truck, a stool, a bench, and a "stove" against the wall—no chimney. This room was the only apartment occupied by this family. Here, in this room, was done every household duty. Five other compartments, similar to this once, completed the "house." The other compartments were occupied by five other families. There were low partitions between the rooms and the smoke from all the cooking, with all the mingled odors, circulated freely.

And while our doctor was treating this man, and thought that he had the "case" as his own, the man was taking all sorts of treatment from any and every sort of source from which he was led to expect benefit of any kind. The case certainly was desperate.

The man got into that condition just as every sinner gets under the condemnation of eternal death—by his own transgression. But the problem just at this time for us was not how he got into this condition, but how to get him out of it. The grace of God is sufficient for the worst of sinners and his mercy reached to this man and gave him at least a little more time to prepare for eternity. I don't remember what the treatment was that Dr. Page gave the man—I rather think he lanced the abscess, however—but I do remember that some time afterwards, when we thought that the man must surely have died and been consigned to his fathers, we met him alive and rapidly recovering.

We left Igatpuri soon afterward, and I never hard what became of this patient later. But we were in India long enough to learn that this sort of treatment is by no means uncommon. Oh, for the power to replace it all with the kind of treatment prompted by the religion of Jesus Christ.

The kind word or look, the gentle touch, the cleanly care, of the ordinary missionary do much to relieve suffering in a land where unsanitary conditions, filth, burning with hot irons, and other barbarous treatment mark the common method of dealing with every form of disease. How much more, then, will be accomplished by the skilled hands of the Christian physician who witnesses for his Master in every contact with the suffering ones.

CHAPTER 11

HOW GOSAIN BECAME A CHRISTIAN

What is a Gosian?

It is the name of a caste of Hindus and is applied to the member of that caste.

Most people nowadays know that there are four castes of Hindus in India: priests, soldiers, merchants, and laborers; that these castes are divided and subdivided into many castes, and that there are many people who are not even in the four castes but are outcast. It is thought by the Hindus that all men must have a priest by whom they may approach their gods and that there is no way of coming near their gods except through the priest. But the Brahmin, as the priest is called, needs a priest for himself, and how will he manage? The Hindu system provides the Gosain, who is a priest to the priests. He is above the Brahmin in the scale of the Hindu system.

In the rainy season of 1902 work was begun on the buildings at Rudri, the second station of the American Mennonite Mission. Having had the experience of beginning work at one station before, we decided to improve

*Orphan boys at Dhamtari, India, performing
their morning ablutions at the well.*

the opportunity offered us to bring the word of God to the people at the very first. Every morning the work people were gathered in front of the little building where the missionary lived and where the office and headquarters for the station were. The Gospel of Mark in Chhattisgarhi was about the only book available in that language, the language spoken by the common people in the vicinity of Dhamtari. The Chhattisgarhi dialect has about the same relation to Hindi as Pennsylvania Dutch has to High German. This was the scripture that was read to the people in the morning worship. One morning, soon after the work had been begun, the missionary asked the people if they understood the reading. One woman spoke up with a cheerful look and voice, "Kai bar na samjhe? Ye ham are boil hai." (Why should we not understand? This is our speech.)

Among the workmen who gathered there was one young Gosain by the name of Bisrampuri. He was an active, muscular man, and soon proved his usefulness as an unskilled workman. His intelligence won him a place of favor and he was given little responsibilities as they came within the range of his capacity.

About two years later this Bisrampur came to one of the missionaries and said, "I want to be a Christian." "What? you want to be a Christian?" "Yes." "But you are a Gosain. Your friends will persecute you. You will lose your caste. Think of all that it will mean to you." "I have thought it out and I have decided. I know that there is no salvation outside of Jesus Christ and I want to be saved."

Then followed a long conversation in which it came out that Bisrampur's first knowledge of Jesus Christ was obtained from those little meetings in which Chhattisgarhi Gospel of Mark was read. He secretly believed it then and later made the great decision. That conversation was about Wednesday. On Saturday evening the village owner met Bisrampuri at the little market place near the mission bungalow. He said to him, "Bisrampuri, I hear you want to become a Christian." "Yes, it is true." "Well, if you wish to, but know this, you will not live three months if you do; or, if you should live three months, you certainly will not live six months."

There was a threat implied in this as well as prediction. It was as much as to say, "We'll see to it that you do not live so long as that."

Bisrampuri said little but assured those who asked him that he fully knew what he was doing and that he had to look out for his own salvation and was doing what he knew he must do if he wished to be saved. His mother was a widow. His oldest brother was dead, and his second brother had gone to take of the ashes of the father and brother (for all orthodox Hindus who can afford to burn their dead) to the sacred shrine of Jaggernaut at Puri and Bisrampuri was the sold support of his mother. She had delayed making marriage arrangements for her son, but when she heard of his intention to become a follower of Christ she hurriedly began preparations to get him married and thus put a barrier in his way of becoming a Christian. All this did not change his resolution.

On Sunday morning he was baptized. His mother had taken everything from him except one loin cloth. He had borrowed a vest to come to the church. In that clothing he was received. No shoes, no head dress, his arms and legs bare, nothing in the world he could call his own but his loin cloth. His mother had even taken the wages he had received for the past week.

After he had been baptized, and we were about to kneel in prayer, I saw Bisrampur's mother come in at the back door of the building, cross over and sit down. From the words used in the prayer, she knew that the deed had been done and that her son was separated from her religion forever. Nothing he could do could ever restore him to his caste.

After the close of the service, the mother went out quickly, but waited for us outside our bungalow. When we arrived she poured out a volley of abuse and filthy language such as I never heard before or since. She went home after a while, but she was bitter against us and against anyone who helped her son in his new religion.

Bisrampuri well knew the danger he was in and for a time kept very close to the home of one of our Christians. After a time his mother's anger seemed to cool off a little and she began to invite her son to come to visit her. We warmed him to be very careful as to his eating and drinking when he was in his mother's home. For a knowledge of poisonous medicines the Indian had taken the master's degree. Bisrampuri himself knew the danger and was careful. Many a convert to Christianity had gone home to his heathen or Mohammedan parents and taken one meal or one drink and come away to die a slow and lingering death or else to become a raving maniac for life.

After many months Bisrampuri 's mother seemed quite reconciled. She frequently called to see the missionaries and at Bisrampuri 's home, for he in the meantime had been married to one of the orphanage girls.

One day, while he was at his mother's home and felt hungered, she repeated her invitation to take some food. He took only a little. It tasted queer and his suspicion was aroused. As it was he got enough of the poison to make him sick for some months. At last he recovered. No charge could be made for the evidence is too meager to convict. But there is moral certainty of guilt nevertheless. His own mother had tried to poison him because he became a Christian!

All those things took place about ten years ago. The last we heard of Bisrampuri was that he was a faithful colporter and evangelist and was going from village to village bearing the message of the Redeemer for whom he gave literally all that he had.

Has our religion cost any of us nearly as much as that? Would we be willing, and even anxious, when we consider all that Jesus Christ has done for us.

CHAPTER 12

LEPROUS MANTURA AND HER SISTER

Leprosy is a dreadful disease. In its most common form it attacks the entire body but is mainly manifest in the extremities. The ends of the fingers and toes become sore, the nails drop off, and gradually the fingers and toes are eaten away by the disease. Under proper conditions of cleanliness, the sores often heal and there is the appearance of an amputated limb. But there is no remedy known for the cure of the disease. The leper knows that he is doomed to die slowly, very slowly, not by inches, but by minute fractions of an inch. Often the disease breaks out in the eyes and nose, and sometimes even the ears are eaten away.

But I started to tell about Mantura.

Mantura was far along in the stages of leprosy. Her fingers and toes were all gone. Half her palms were wasted away, and her feet were mere stumps. Even her thumbs were gone, and the only way she could grasp anything was by bringing her two palms together. The disease had attacked her eyes and she was totally blind.

A Typical Leper

But in the midst of her afflictions, Mantura had found a source of infinite joy. She had found peace in Christ Jesus and He had healed her soul.

One day, while Brother Lapp was visiting the Leper Asylum in his work as superintendent, Mantura said she had a request and she was told to speak on.

"Sahib (Sir), I should like to go out to my village to see my sister." (You remember that she is totally blind.)

"Where does your sister live?"

"In Gatisilli."

"How far is that from here?"

"It will be ten or twelve kos" (about twenty-five miles), spoke up several of the lepers.

"But how could you ever get there?"

"I'd walk."

"But how would you find the way?"

"Well, you send Dasoda (a non-leprous attendant) along with the other women when they go to their villages, why could she not go with me?"

"But what would you want out there in the village at that rate?"

"Why, here in the Leper Asylum I have learned to know Jesus, and He gives me so much joy in my heart that I want to tell my sister about Him too. I know that she had never hard of Him, and I want to tell her how happy I am."

That was a pretty strong argument and the missionary began to relent.

"How long will it take you?"

"Oh, about 10 days."

So it was arranged. Dasoda could not grasp the hand of Mantura to guide her way, for no leper is allowed to touch a clean person, so she took one end of the long staff in her hand and Mantura grasped the other end of the staff between her two stumps of palms and hobbled along on her stumps of feet until at last they reached the village of Gatisilli.

She "saw" her sister, or did that which was better, and told her the story of the precious Jesus as she heard it in the Leper Asylum. For the first time in her life the sister heard the precious Name. She had not even heard it in profanity. Truly these people know not the Lord.

And they came back the same way as they went, slowly, slowly, and got back to the Asylum before the expiration of the ten days.

Some time after that, Mantura became very sick. I think she had pneumonia. We thought and she thought she was gong to die. Again we called the Asylum. Brother Lapp asked her, "How do you feel, Mantura?"

"Oh, I have so very much pain," she said between her groans.

"But how is it in your heart (soul)?"

"Oh, I am so happy in my soul."

"Why?"

"I am soon going to go to be with Jesus, and I'll have no more pain."

It was not death to her! It was going into the presence of Jesus, her Lord.

But Mantura did not die at that time. She recovered of her acute illness, and the following year she again asked and obtained permission to visit her village and "see" her sister. And for the second time in her life, that sister heard the precious message of the love of Jesus.

Once a year a sermon by a poor, blind, crippled, leper woman!

Do you think the church would grow rapidly in that village? And yet God has used messengers for His Word with less promise according to our way of looking at matters than had the loving heart of Mantura.

Worth while to teach the lepers?

The story of Mantura is one example among many and it will be sufficient answer to the question.

Those things took place some ten or eleven years ago and Mantura has since gone to be really with her Savior. But her testimony remains here on earth, while her happy soul praises the blessed Redeemer who bought her.

And I am glad to tell, too, that a sub-station of the Mision has been opened at Gatisilli and now the people of that village have daily opportunity of hearing the Gospel message. Mantura's faith and prayer are being rewarded.

CHAPTER 13

WHEN CHAINTU WENT TO SLEEP

As this book has been written mostly for young people, I don't suppose that many of the readers of this story have trouble about sleep, either in not being able to sleep at the time they should be sleeping, or in being able to keep awake when that is the proper thing to do. Most people who are well and live properly have little trouble with their sleeping. I know of some people who had trouble about going to sleep in church when the preacher is preaching. I guess it's because they got to bed too late the night before— or some other reason— for they really want to stay awake and hear what is being said but they—just—get s-l-e-e-p-y—and the next thing they know the sermon is all over and they know very little about what the preacher said.

Sleep is a most excellent thing in its place and at the proper time. "He giveth his beloved sleep," is what the psalmist says, and there is a very precious thing to remember in connection with sleep. It is when we sleep in the cool, fresh air of night, with the windows open to God's great

store-house of oxygen out-of-doors, that we gain the vitality we lost in our work or play during the busy day.

But what has that to do with Chaintu? Chaintu means "the man of rest." I used to think he had the right name, for he liked to rest better than anything else. One day I found him resting up on the scaffold at the new bungalow at Rudri, fast asleep, while the others were working, and he should have been working too.

But this is not the time I was going to tell you about.

Chaintu was one of the Christians at Dhamtari. Poor fellow! I believe he went back to Hindusim for a while. I don't know whether he came into the church again and made a confession of his wrong or not. I know that Chaintu needed Jesus as his Savior and he was once on a fair way of being a good and noble Christian, but I really believe that his disposition to take rest at improper times led to his downfall.

I can't show you a picture of Chaintu, but we have a picture of the audience who were in church where he went to sleep. Yes, it was in church where he went to sleep that time! This picture was not taken on that day, but on another day, not Sunday, but the people before the minister were just about the same that day as on the day when the picture was taken. Chaintu never like to sit on a chair or bench but always sat on the floor with his back against the wall over to the left.

Chaintu had a brother-in-law. I have been trying to think of his name, but somehow Indian names do slip out of memory after so many years as we have been out of India. I think his name was Tetkhu, but that doesn't matter. On the day that Chaintu went to sleep his brother-in-law was wide awake and listening to the sermon with both ears and all his mind. I must explain that in India it is often the practice for the preacher to stop preaching and teach his audience as if it were a class in school. He will ask questions and the audience will answer just as they do in school. In this way he can find out whether they understand or not.

I was preaching on the text, "Awake thou that sleepiest." (Eph. 5:14), in Hindi, of course, and had made the introductory explanation about the blessings of sleep and how good a thing it is that God gives us sleep; how the disciples were to watch when Jesus prayed, how they went to sleep, and what they lost by that sleep; how that sometimes persons who went to sleep were even punished with death for sleeping when the lives of so many others depended on their keeping awake. I was just going to make the proper applications regarding spiritual sleep; how dangerous it is to sleep spiritually and how Christ can give us the life we need to keep wakeful. I stopped for a moment, looked around for closer attention, then said, "Wah jo sota hai, so kaun hai?" (He who sleeps, who is he?)

As I said, Chaintu's brother-in-law was in the audience. He was awake. He was sitting over against the wall near Chaintu. He had been making observations on his own account. He had seen my pause. He had heard me ask who it is who is asleep. And he felt sure he could answer that question. So in a loud, clear voice he answered, "Chaintu!" And he was quite right in his answer! Chaintu was fast asleep at his favorite place against the wall.

You may well guess, I paused again. I looked around and saw where the answer came from. Chaintu also heard his name mentioned and was awakening. The children saw the situation and although they are very artful never to laugh and hardly to smile in church, a good many of them bit their lips hard to keep from laughing out loud. Others took in the situation, and began to wish for some kind of relief for their feelings.

Don't ask me what the preacher did! But the rest of the sermon was not so long that day as it had been planned, and I am afraid its spiritual applications were lost to a large extent in thoughts of how to keep awake in church.

As this story began with a moral, I will let you make your own moral at the end.

CHAPTER 14

BITTEN BY
A MAD JACKAL

Night had settled over the quiet compound at the American Mennonite Mission in Dhamtari. It was a dark, moonless, cloudy, misty night, the night of August 17, 1906. The wall on the west side of the compound had been broken and the partial repair served to keep out cattle but not to keep out smaller animals. A few days before this poor, crippled Bisayan had died. Her room-mate had been a girl named Janki, who was almost blind. After the death of Bisayan, Janki felt lonely and said she could not bear to sleep in the room where her friend had closed her eyes in death. So that night found her sleeping on the verandah wrapped in her blanket.

The missionaries went to their rest that night little thinking of danger. About half-past one Brother and Sister M.C. Lapp were awakened by piercing shrieks from the region of the girl's hospital. Thinking nothing of his own danger, Brother Lapp rushed out in his pajamas and found Janki screaming and waving her hands over her head. She was too nearly blind to flee from danger or to defend herself. By the dim light of the lantern

The verandah of a missionary's house. Under the most ideal conditions life in India is difficult for an American, so the verandah is not luxury but an absolute necessity.

that was standing on the floor of the verandah, Brother Lapp say that Janki's face was covered with blood. He hastened to pick up the lantern and found Jhariarin, a faithful girl who had been very helpful in caring for the sick, standing in the doorway also screaming and trying to cover her face with her sari or dress. He spoke to Jhariarin, and asked her what was the matter. She had no time to catch her breath to answer until Brother Lapp felt the sharp fangs of an animal snap him in the thigh.

Unconsciously he struck at the animal with his hand that held the lantern and it left him for a moment. Then he hurried toward the bungalow for his gun. He was not gone long, but imagine his agony as he heard by the cries of poor blind Janki that she was being attacked again. As he ran Brother Lapp called the night watchman, who soon afterwards came with a lantern. He also called to the girls to get inside their rooms quickly and close all doors.

Having secured his gun he came toward the place where the jackal, as it proved to be, had been. Seeing him come with the lantern, the rabid beast left the girl and came toward Brother Lapp. In the excitement his aim was not true and he either missed the animal altogether or wounded it but slightly. But the shot disconcerted the animal sufficiently to allow all the girls to get under cover.

Our baby Ruth was the about two-and-a-half months old. She had been awake about the time of the first scream of the girls but had gone to sleep again. Both her parents were still awake when the shot was fired. It was sufficiently common to shoot at some prowling dog that this caused no special uneasiness. But a few minutes later the telephone rang for our bungalow. Still unalarmed, I went at once, though deliberately, across the verandah toward the sitting rom, where the telephone was. Before I got to it, however, Sister Schertz had answered the call, and when she saw me she called in excited tones, "O brother Ressler! Come in quickly. Sarah (Sister M.C. Lapp) says that there is a mad jackal in the compound and that he is biting the girls, that he had bitten Mahlon (M.C. Lapp), who wants you to come over." Then listening for further instructions, she added, "They want you to put on your heaviest clothes and not to come out without a lantern and a gun." Then you may be sure that I was wide awake.

The Sundarganj bungalows are built at opposite sides of the five acre compound. Between them is a long line of what were at the time orphanage buildings. There was a driveway about the middle of the orphanage building through which we had to pass to go from one bungalow to the other.

Both guns were in the other bungalow. I followed directions as nearly as I could, took the lantern, dressed with heavy clothing including gloves, and armed myself with prayer and a heavy club that we always kept handy for chance snakes that night become disagreeably friendly.

As I passed around the end of the orphanage building, Bother Lapp called to me from near his bungalow to come to him quickly as the jackal was somewhere near where I was. I went quickly.

By that time there was not a sleeping eye on the compound except, perhaps those of the babies. We held a rapid consultation. Burning out the wounds with permanganate of potash was the first step in treating the bites. There was not a bit of the medicine in the bungalow where we were. We had some of it in our bungalow at one end of the compound, but there was more of it at the hospital at the other end of the compound. We decided to go to our bungalow. With two guns and two lanterns we got safely across without seeing the jackal.

We cauterized Brother Lapp's wounds deeply with the permanganate and held another rapid consultation. The next duty was to treat the wounds of the girls similarly. In order to reach them we had to cross the compound again in the deep darkness with no telling where that mad jackal was prowling. If we had ever lacked an example of watching and prayer before that night we got the perfect example then. We didn't speak. There was nothing to say. But our hearts were in touch with the Infinite every moment of the way. Just as we came around the corner of the orphanage building I saw the brute going at right angles with our path not over ten steps away from us. "There he goes." I said very quietly. "Where?" "Just ahead of us." Mahlon stopped to set his lantern down and I raised mine under the gun, Both guns reported at the same instant and then all was black with smoke for a few seconds. Then Mahlon's sharp eyes saw through the gloom and he cried out, "He's down!" Then turning to our bungalow he shouted, "Praise the Lord! The jackal's killed."

There was no thought of sleep for most of us the rest of the night. The girls in the orphanage kept singing all the time until daybreak to keep up their courage.

After the danger was past and the wounded had been treated, we had time to hear the story of how it happened from the girls. Jhariarin was awakened from her sleep by the screams of Janki and, brave girl that she was went to the rescue. She saw the animal in the dim light and thought it was a dog. She at once began striking it with her hands, for she had no weapon. The jackal left Janki and attacked Jhariarin, biting her once on the nose and inside the upper lip. She threw her cloth over her face and stumbled in at the door, her foot extended. Then the jackal bit her on the calf of the leg and followed her into the room. A lame girl inside procured a brass pot and beat the animal on the head with it and thus got it out. Then Brother Lapp came on the scene and was bitten.

A jackal is a species of wolf, about the size of the collie, and much like the coyote of our western plains in its howl and its habits. It is usually timid and afraid of people, but when rabid it is like all other mad animals—it is fearless and snaps at all within reach. It feeds on carrion and frequently digs up human remains from the shallow graves in which they are often buried. Because of its feeding habits, the bite of a jackal is very poisonous and the bite of a mad jackal is much more deadly than that of a mad dog.

We sent for the two qualified medical men of Dhamtari and told them what we had done. They said that we had done all they could have done and that the only thing now was to go to Kasauli, away up in the Himalayas, eight hundred miles away, to be treated at the Paseur Institute at that place.

No need to tell the story of the journey, interesting as that was, for it is not a part of what interested us most now. The treatment at the Institute was successful and three patients fully recovered and never developed any of the symptoms of the dreaded disease. But while the awful experience was being passed through, many serious thoughts came to the missionaries.

If these lines should fall into the hands of those who are responsible for the sending out of new missionaries or into the hands of some who have inclinations to think that "it would be nice to be a missionary some day," the following, written under the shadow of the Himalayas and just after that awful night, may be of interest.

"O you brethren with whom rests the responsibly for the sending of workers, stop, think, pray! Send workers now! Not a dozen. Only two each year, or perhaps four. Not those you can spare at home—they can be spared here too. Not those who would be afraid to come where they hear that cholera, small-pox, leprosy, mad jackals and dogs, scorpions, and deadly snakes are sometimes on our compound or even in our very houses. Those who are afraid of such things are not the stuff missionaries are made of.

"Send workers now! Then it will never happen that you will be looking around for someone to send when the workers should be already on the field, prepared and experienced, ready to take up the responsibility someone else is compelled for a time to lay down.

"Pray for us in a way that will tell so that not only can we feel the influence of your prayers in spirit, but that even the heathen can see the results of your prayers."

CHAPTER 15

WATCHING FOR A TIGER

Natives of India are not allowed to have fire arms except certain classes, and those are required to have license from the Government. It is undoubtedly a wise provision on the part of the powers that be, for the number of Englishmen who hold sway in India is pitiably small as compared with the Indians. The great mass of the people are ignorant and are easily led by any one who can talk glibly and has a bit of force to his character. The demagogues of India are many and they are smooth of tongue. They can out-talk the foreigner ten to one. Experience has shown England that if there is unbounded opportunity, the wiley Indian will mislead the innocent and ignorant Indian into insurrection—with his own gain in view and the destruction of both the poor Indian subject and the English ruler as his ultimate object.

So very few Native Indians have guns.

As a result of this, the wild beasts of the forest have an easy time of it. Deer are abundant in the forests and on the plains. Wild hogs are

Banana grove at the Leper Asylum near Dhamtari, India

so numerous in places that they do great damage to the growing crops. And the animals which feed on these grain and grass eating animals are also abundant. There are tigers and various kinds of leopards, and from these magnificent beasts on down to hyenas, jackals, and foxes there are all shades and gradations of flesh-eating creatures. The government tries to limit the killing of deer in places where tigers and leopards are known to live, lest the destruction of the natural food of these big felines would drive them to attack the village people. And from village cattle to village people as food for tigers, the step is not a long one.

As American missionaries have the privilege of owning guns, they come to be looked upon as the natural protectors of the Natives against the ravages of wild beasts. This would seem a strange office for a minister of the Gospel to fill, but from what has been said, it will easily be seen how it has come to pass.

This story is about a tiger. I have constantly to keep the subject in mind or I will go off and tell about the bear that they watched for from trees on the bank of a reservoir (tank), and saw, and didn't shoot. Or the hyena that we tied up a goat for. And when we came Brother Lapp shot him before he got to the goat. Or the big macher deo, or spotted tiger, that killed a village heifer and we watched for him and saw him and shot at him but missed. Those were all very interesting at the time, but they are not the story of the tiger.

One morning very early as some of the carts from our village of Balodgahan were going along the road through the jungles, suddenly a big, striped "Royal Bengal Tiger," as they call him in the zoo, came out of the woods and jumped upon the back of one of the oxen in the cart and began to gnaw the back of the ox's neck as a cat would would bite the neck of a big rat. The driver beat the tiger on the head with his driving stick, but the tiger was too interested in his game to notice such a trifle and held fast to the ox until it ceased to struggle. Then it went away and lay down in the tall grass.

The men dragged the cart away with the other ox and sent word in to the missionaries.

Now, a tiger usually kills his game one night and eats it the following day, allowing it to "ripen" in the sun during the day. If he is very hungry he may eat a little at once after killing the animal, but he never comes back to his kill after having eaten his fill on the second night. During the day after killing an animal he usually lies asleep within a furlong of the place where the animal lies. Dogs, jackals, and other animals that live on carrion, will not touch the carcass during the first day. They wait until the tiger has had his full meal. Then they come and, with much quarreling and noise, finish up all edible portions.

In this case the missionaries began to make preparations to do their duty. They had two boards tied up in two trees about twenty feet from the ground. As evening came on, they went to the trees and took several natives with them. One or two natives went that should have remained at home. On one board in one tree was a missionary and two trusty natives. On the other tree were a missionary and three natives. Whether they were all as trusty as they should have been is still an open question. They had their guns ready and they watched. On the one tree they thought they heard the tiger coming. The one native still claims that he saw him, On the other tree the missionary was doing his best. But there were four men on the one board. One of the natives got uncomfortable. He had been waiting a long time, he thought, and was getting sleepy. He changed his position rather forcibly—and the rope that held up the board broke. Time of all times for such an accident!

Down came the four men, loaded and cocked guns, board and all, in a heap. The tiger had not expected any such conduct on the part of the trees. He seems to have had a bit of natural politeness about him and quietly withdrew until the other folks had time to adjust themselves.

What were the other watchers to do? For all they knew the men who fell might have been badly hurt. The only thing to do was to get down and examine the damages. Providentially, there was no harm done to any of the men but it would have been useless to climb that tree again in the sight of the waiting tiger, and the only thing to be done was to go home.

After the men had gone, the tiger came and finished his meal in peace. Then the jackals and hyenas came for their share, and the next morning a few bones told the sad tale of an oxen and a tiger.

Tigers come sometimes when they are not being looked for. One evening Brother M.C. Lapp was riding along a short-cut path in the woods on his bicycle. All at once he saw a tiger standing in the path a short distance ahead. The tiger looked as much surprised as Brother Lapp felt. He had seen men before, perhaps even white men with queer dress and big hats; but this thing that glided so smoothly along was new to him. And when Brother Lapp gave the big bell on the bicycle a vigorous ring, it was entirely too much for even a tiger. Off he bounded as fast as he could and the missionary went peacefully on his way.

Hindus worship all animals, but some are considered more sacred than others. The cow is considered especially sacred. One would think that, therefore, the tiger which kills a cow would be slain by the worshipper of the cow. But, as a matter of fact, the life of the tiger is respected as much as that of the cow. The Hindu believes that when a person dies, his soul passes into some other person just born, or into some other animal. All the animals are supposed to have souls of some person who lived in the past. In killing an animal a person always fears he might kill one of his ancestors. So, no faithful Hindu would kill even a tiger to save his own life. I might explain that not all Indians are Hindus. Many belong to classes outside the castes, many are Mohammedans, and even many who claim to be Hindus are not faithful to their religion and would have no scruples against taking animal life. They are glad to have a missionary kill a tiger, for then they do not feel responsible.

With such a belief the Hindu has no hope in the immortality of the soul—that blessed joy of the Christian. Salvation to the Hindu means only a deliverance from being born again into some other form of life. What a joy it is to be delivered from such a state of darkness and to see the light which Christ can give.

CHAPTER 16

SNAKES IN THE BUNGALOW

Day before yesterday I was talking to a young man in India. He seemed very much interested and asked a good many questions. At last he said, "I often thought I'd like to take a trip over there myself."

Was that all? Only a trip to the Orient?

Well , there are a good many people who are willing to pay good, hard-earned money of their own in order that they may take a trip to the far eastern countries. But that is not what takes a true missionary to the heathen lands. He is interested in the souls of the poor people who are going to their death without a knowledge of the way of salvation. There are many exciting stories a missionary might tell about the dangerous things in tropical countries, but those things have no souls to save. When he consents to tell such a story, it is with a view of showing the kind of lives missionaries have to live in order that they may be used in bringing the knowledge of Christ to the lost ones.

Poisonous reptiles are one of the sources of danger. Scorpions are

*And Indian tonga, the ordinary conveyance for business
or pleasure in the vicinity of Dhamtari.*

abundant in the region of the American Mennonite Mission, and they are especially plentiful in the rainy season. The sting of the scorpion is on the end of the tail and is shaped somewhat like a toe and claw of a cat, the claw representing the sting and the soft ball of the toe representing the poison bag. When a scorpion strikes a person, a single wound is made and the effect is rather more severe than the strain of the bumble-bee.

A poisonous snake has two long grooved fangs in the roof of its mouth. The poison sac is in the upper jaw. When it strikes, its mouth is opened wide and the fangs are plunged into the flesh while the poison flows along the grooves of the fangs. These fangs are not proper teeth and when they are not used as weapons, they lie harmless along the roof of the mouth. A snake bite leaves two wounds near together. In this way a snake bite can be distinguished from the scorpion's sting. It is important to know this. Our missionaries have frequently successfully treated bites from poisonous snakes by lancing each fang wound, letting it bleed freely, then rubbing into the wounds crystals of permanganate of potash as an antiseptic.

In the rainy season snakes come out of the hiding places they have occupied during the hot season, and often seek shelter in houses and stables. One evening two of our missionary sisters were sitting in their room reading by lamp light. One of them occupied an arm chair made with split bamboos. As she read, she caught "from the corner of her eye" a little movement in the arm of the chair. She looked and saw that a small snake had wound itself into the sticks of the arm and had evidently meant no harm but had been disturbed by the movement of the other occupant of the chair.

She did not hesitate a moment, nor dispute the possession of the chair with the reptile, but got up at once. The snake left the chair too; evidently as much frightened as the missionary.

Why, yes; of course the ladies screamed! Both of them. What would you expect a pair of ladies to do if a snake suddenly was found in the room? The men folks of the household promptly came to the rescue, but before they had arrived one of the sisters had gotten a board and punched the life out of the snake just as it was going over the doorsill.

The native authorities who came to examine the victim pronounced it a full-grown snake whose bite was deadly. And we were all grateful to our kind heavenly Father for His gracious deliverance.

Some time later, one of these sisters was occupying a temporary hut with the girls of the orphanage, when they had gone to the country on account of plague in the town of Dhamtari. One day they saw a snake up in the grass roof. They tried to kill it there, but it fell down on the bed and was lost among the covers. They hunted and hunted, but saw nothing more of the serpent. I've often thought of the courage of that missionary. She went to sleep in that bed that very night and slept soundly the night though.

Our bathroom had one door opening into the sleeping room and one opening on the verandah. One evening I went into the bathroom, and the outside door refused to close properly. I pulled it open again and something dropped on the floor of the verandah. I banged the doors shut, but in my haste did not close them tightly, and rushed into the sleeping room to get the heavy cane which we always kept handy. The snake was circling about on the verandah. It had evidently been lying on the top of the doors and I had injured it somewhat in closing the doors. My good wife held the lamp inside the screen and I went out and did battle. Before I got it killed, the snake was in the bathroom again. Finally a blow took proper effect and the animal remained quiet long enough for me to finally dispatch it. It proved to be four and a-half feet long and was called a ghora karait. Its bite is considered quite poisonous.

There are many nonpoisonous snakes in India too—great pythons are twelve to fifteen feet long, and even longer. They are hard on chicken roosts at times. Just after they shed their skin they are very hungry. After they have eaten they are sluggish and can easily be captured and are apt to show no disposition to fight. Brother M.C. Lapp had one of those pythons in a box for quite a long time. One time, after it had sloughed its skin, and did not get its feed of live rats as son as it wanted it, it broke from its cage and got into a native woman's dwelling where she had her chickens, and killed a number of them. Brother Lapp saw that there was no use trying to capture it and shot it.

But with all the poisonous things about, I have never heard of a missionary being fatally bitten by any of them. Brother Lehman among our own workers, and others that we could name, can testify as to how the sting of a scorpion feels. But I have never heard of such a sting being fatal. The bare feet of the natives are the most commonly bitten portion of the body. Besides, they usually sleep on the ground. A snake is passing harmlessly, an arm is thrown out in sleep, and the snake feels it to be a challenge and strikes. The use of bed stands, shoes and stockings would greatly lessen the number of deaths from snakes among natives.

Brother Lapp was once called to a village about a mile off to treat a girl who had been bitten while herding cattle. She could not have been bitten more than two hours before he arrived. But before he got to the place she was quite dead.

Knowing the deadly nature of the bite of the cobra, karait, and other serpents, we cannot but feel that a kind Providence watches over the lives of those who hold His name in reverence, and tell His message of salvation to others.

CHAPTER 17

EXPERIENCES WITH SMALL PESTS

Great size is not essential in a creature in order that it may be very annoying or very destructive. Persistence and numbers go a long way to offset lack in size.

Among the small pests of India I should not hesitate to give the chief place to a little insect commonly called in English the white ant, though it is no ant at all, but a termite. This creature illustrates two familiar Scripture texts. Like the poor, it is always "with you," while you live in the tropics, and never for a day will you be allowed to relax your vigilance if you wish to preserve your most precious documents from destruction. And it loves darkness rather than light because its deeds are evil. It works under cover. If you wish to see a crowd of excited "white ants" just knock down the mud covering under which they are at work. They scurry under cover just as fast as their tiny legs can carry them.

Out on the plain the white ants build their nests in literal hills. These mounds are often as much as ten or fifteen feet high and six feet

*A village school in hare of the American Mennonite Mission
near Dhamtari, India. The boys are ready for their calisthenic drill.*

across. Far down under ground, with innumerable passages leading to her royal chamber, is the queen of the ant-hill. Her body as grown to such an enormous size that her legs are lifted clear off the floor. Her only work is to lay the eggs that produce more white ants and she is carefully fed by her worker ants.

But it is when the ant colony takes a fancy to sharing your living quarters that they become of chief interest to you. When you built your house and did not dig a cellar, for the cellar would turn into a pestilential pool of water in the rainy seasons, so it happens that underneath your cemented floor may be the nucleus of several white ant colonies. You build of brick or stone laid in mud and plastered with mortar of lime and sand. With a view to economy in space you have placed several cupboards with shelves in the walls and partitions. On the shelves you have stored your precious library.

One morning when you are particular busy, you notice on the lower corner of one of these cupboards a streak of dried mud. You hastily brush it down, and, if you are new to the country, you will be glad you gotten rid of the dirt and go on with your work as per program. If experience has made you wise, you will drop everything else and proceed at once to see where that streak of dirt ends. Most likely it will be found to lead right to your books. You try to pull one of them out. It sticks tight. You pull hard. When it at last yields to your force, you will find it covered with mud, the cover partly eaten, and you are fortunate if there is not a hole pierced right through the heart of the book. The extent of the damage is limited only by the length of time the insects were allowed to work unhindered. And the only visible sign of their ravages before you began to investigate was that little streak of dried mud under which the ants worked and traveled.

How deep they go I do not know, but I know that they must go to water, for they can work only as they soak the dirt into a plastic condition with water. Their work often involves the ruin of all the wood work of a large dwelling house. An application of coal tar discourages them but even that does not secure safety, for if they find one little point uncoated, they will work their way through that spot and devour to the extent of their desire. Wood, paper, and leather are their favorite diet. Glass, stone and metals are safe.

Soon after we arrived in India we visited a large book-selling establishment in Allahabad. We had heard of white ants and asked the manager about them. Was there no remedy? He sadly shook his head. "No, nothing but eternal vigilance."

When it comes to the selection of the second place among the small pests of India, the difficulties of the task multiply. And the difficulties are not all over when you have named a dozen or more that each have claims to your notice. When you are in India you not only name the troublesome creatures—you sit up and take notice.

For purposes of Indian conversation it may be all right to speak of "B-flats" and "F-sharps," for those are supposedly polite terms well understood. Should any chance Indian reader see these pages, he will kindly pardon the use of plain English for the sake of American readers. For their sake we must say plainly "bed-bugs" and "fleas."

The importance these two pests occupy in the economy of Indian life may partly be imagined when it is stated that a government commission, after long and thorough investigation, reported that the flea is responsible for the dissemination of the dreaded plague through the agency of rats. Or perhaps it would be more exact to say that rats spread the disease through the medium of fleas. And bed-bugs, well, the price of immunity from them is the same as the immunity from white ants—eternal vigilance. The superstitious Indian surrenders. It is against his religion to take life and the bugs multiply rapidly. There are servants and others who come and go in the homes of the missionaries. Unless there is constant watchfulness the pests gain a foot hold—and they have so many feet with which to hold on!

For a time, the large school building at Sundarganj, with its bamboo matting on the roof and bamboo matting on the floor, was occupied by some of the boys as sleeping quarters. Then the "B-flats" flourished! The matting afforded such an excellent hiding place. The bugs got so bad that some of the missionaries actually feared to go to meeting on Sunday on their account.

But the boys rose to the occasion. The matting was taken from the floor. With kettles of hot water and disinfectants they waged valiant warfare agains the invaders, and soon the place could be visited with comfort and a sense of security.

Fleas are not so abundant in the vicinity of Dhamtari as they are in some other places. Where they flourish, they are very hard to exterminate. There was once a conference of missionaries in western India. A very solemn and important matter was under consideration. One elder, to whom the fleas were particularly trying, sitting with his wife in the audience, became conscious of a wicked flea inside his stocking. Quietly he stopped, turned down the sock and cautiously peeped within. His wife, who is the soul of propriety, tried to get him to straighten up and let the flea go without attracting attention. This was quite too much for the patience of the elder. "Do you think I'm going to let the fleas eat me up alive?" he asked indignantly, and quite loud enough to upset the entire solemnity of the occasion.

Head lice also deserve notorious mention. Oh, the discouragements of the conflicts with lice! All too soon the worker was forced into a place of responsibility in the orphanage. It looks smooth on the outside for a time, but one day he discovers there are lice on the heads of his children! Drastic measures are the only remedy. The children are lined up and carefully examined. The supposedly clean are separated from those infected. Coal-oil is freely applied. After a few days the treated patients are examined. Those who are found clean are allowed to go back to the general living quarters. The others are again treated. In course of a few weeks the missionary joyfully announces that he has just released the last louse infected orphan and that the orphanage is now clean!

Alas, alas! next day he sees a suspicious head scratching. He examines the scratched head. And—the details are too harrowing to describe. The announcement is again made that the trouble is as bad as ever—or worse. But the missionary worth the name sticks to his job and does it over and over again.

Mosquitoes also hold a high place among the ranks of the pestiferous in India. They need to be regarded seriously since the pain and annoyance felt when they pay their visits to the tired seeker after rest are not the last nor the greatest of the dangers attending their invasions. It has been well established by observation that the bite of certain mosquitoes carries with it the infection of malarial fever. Persons who have been carefully screened from mosquitoes have escaped fever in districts where the disease was very prevalent among those who were bitten.

For a short time in the coldest weather and for a short time in the hottest weather the mosquitoes do not annoy one very much. During the remainder of the year the only way to secure peaceful rest at night is to sleep under the protection of a mosquito netting. But woe to that careless missionary who tries to sleep without first carefully brushing out every invader. If the edge of the netting has been lifted too long as you got in, or you left one little corner not tucked in—you are just about to lose consciousness when "Cuzzen, cuzzen, cuzzen," comes the all too familiar song in your ear. You wish he'd go and bite some other spot in peace. But no, he must announce his arrival in loud and persistent tones. You strike. But his parting mockery, in a high pitched "No kin!" tells you plainly that you missed. How often this operation is repeated depends on circumstances. Rarely you hit. Oftener you find the assailant in the morning hanging at the top of your netting tent filled with your blood, and he then becomes your easy victim.

There are transient insect pests in other forms. They are bad enough while they last but they do not last long. There are the winged ants that come out in the rains—the mating season—and buzz around the lamps, get into your soup, and make a nuisance of themselves generally. But in a few days they are gone from your presence to work mischief in less prominent places. I shall never forget the flying bugs.

"Flying bugs?"

They are black, hard-winged insects, in shape like the Colorado beetle ("potato bug"), but smaller. They come out in the beginning of the rains.

When disturbed they give out a pungent oder somewhat like the squash bug but much more pronounced.

One evening we had left the lamp burning on the dresser in the bedroom and gone to supper. When we came back we found hundreds of these "flying bugs" all about the lamp and over the dresser. In alarm Memsahib took her handkerchief and began to brush them off. I warned her to not be so fast, but she asked in dismay how we were going to sleep with all those bugs in the rom. Then she smelled the handkerchief. The scent of the bugs was there!

We put the lamp outside for a few minutes and every one of the bugs followed it. Then we shut the door and had peace.

The successful missionary looks upon all those things as a means of grace. If there were no other use for the insect pests they would certainly be useful for the cultivation of patience. And the missionary who does not learn in some way or other to surmount the hindrances these small destroyers of peace place in his way must eventually give up the fight—a failure. The life of the successful missionary is not one long holiday. The more pleasantly he meets his insect enemies, other things equal, the more successful will be his missionary life.

CHAPTER 18

AN ELEPHANT RIDE

Off to the southeast of Raipur, some hundred and twenty-five miles away, without any railway communication, in the Native State of Kariar. At the time of the famine of 1900 the old raja of Kariar was dead, the young raja was a minor, and the state was under the control of the Court of Wards with the Deputy Commissioner of Raipur District as administrator.

Among the chattels of the State of Kariar, when it fell under the control of the Court of Wards, was an elephant.

As the old raja was dead and the young raja too little to use an elephant and elephants are useful creatures, it came to pass that the elephant belonging to the State of Kariar was brought to Raipur for the use of the Deputy Commissioner.

As events in the famine of 1900 moved their weary months along, the Assistant Commissioner in charge of famine arrangements in and about Dhamtari needed an elephant to go about after his work and the Kariar elephant was placed at his disposal, with mahout, howdah, and complete equipment.

An Elephant Ride

When the American Mennonite Mission came to be absorbed in the rainy season duties of the famine relief measures, the one lone missionary then under the jurisdiction of the Mission found it exceedingly difficult to get about from village to village to inspect famine kitchens and do other work that was required. Horseback proved impracticable for the countryside became a swamp sown in rice. Other ways of transportation were suggested, for those villages simply had to be gotten after. Before they were tried another means was provided.

About this time the Assistant Commissioner went to Calcutta on sick leave. He left his camp, including the elephant, in charge of the "American Mennonite Mission" (rather a concentrated mission just then, with one lone missionary) and that was how it happened that I can tell about elephant rides in India.

My first trip on the elephant was made in company with the Assistant Commissioner on a tour of village inspection. The rocking motion, not so very much unlike the motion of a boat in the water, made me very sea sick for a while, but that was a mere incident. On a later ride I took my noon-day nap on the elephant while going from one village to the next.

Howdahs are differently constructed. The one we used was a simple affair. There was a large cushion placed on the animal's back and on this a framework was securely strapped and roped by means of girths. On the frame-work were seating cushions so that the passengers could sit facing each way. There was a foot-rest half way down each side of the elephant. The driver, or mahout as he is called, sat astride the animal's neck and guided the movements of the huge beast by word and by means of a curious iron instrument about a foot long with a handle at one end and two prongs at the other. One prong extended straight in front while the other was bent in the form of a hook.

To turn the elephant right or left the hook was caught on the ear. Hitting it on the head urged it forward. The straight prong was used to punish it for disobedience to orders. But this elephant was very docile and seldom needed anything but the driver's voice to guide it in any direction or to do anything he wished.

We were going along on one of those large banks that divide the rice fields. It was a pretty large bank and probably was a boundary of a village. A little way ahead we noticed a thorny babul (acacia) tree about six inches in diameter at the truck. Its thorny branches would have given us a thorough scratching if we had gone on. It would have been inconvenient for the elephant to get down from the high bank and go around it. We wondered what was to be done.

The mahout calmly went on until we got close to the tree, then he told the elephant to stop. He did so. Then he spoke to the animal in Hindi, "Dub" (Push). The elephant put out its big front foot against the truck of the tree, slowly put its weight on it, and actually pushed it out of the way. The soft condition of the earth, owing to the rains, allowed the roots readily to give way. I admired the elephant very much after that, but I thought perhaps it was just an accident.

A little later we were going along the side of a tank and there was a branch of a tree in such a position that it would have scraped us off if we had gone on. Again the word of command from the mahout stopped the elephant and he said to it, "Phor" (Break). Up went the elephant's trunk around a limb that was not in our way. The mahout spoke to it in Hindi, "Not that one—the other one," in a tone that might be used to a boy that was making some thoughtless blunder about his work. At once the elephant's trunk dropped the limb and took hold of the proper one. In a moment the branch was broken down and the elephant went on peeling off the bark and eating it. My admiration for both mahout and elephant rose several degrees.

But still I thought it might have just happened that way by accident.

Some time later I took a trip through a piece of jungle country with this elephant and driver and such feats were a common occurrence.

Passing along through a rice field the elephant would reach out and pluck bunches of green plants and eat them as we went. Near the corner of the field there was a spot where no rice was growing. This spot was just in our path. The elephant hesitated, eyed the bare spot suspiciously, and seemed to fear that the water there might be uncomfortably deep (you know rice always grows in water). "Go on!" said the mahout, "there is no danger." At once the elephant confidently went ahead. He understood and trusted the driver.

At another time the driver became suspicious and cautioned the animal, "Be careful now; go ahead watching the holes!" The elephant seemed to understand every word. He went very slowly, feeling carefully with its fore feet until it felt the place was safe.

One time the animal seemed discontented. It acted as if it were lame and utter grunts that indicated that it was not comfortable. The driver stopped, got down, and took a piece of wood from between the elephant's toes. Then the mahout got up to his seat astride the neck of the elephant in the usual way, by taking hold of the ears of the beast with each hand, placing one foot in a crook made accommodatingly in the trunk, and then walking on up over the slowly elevated breathing apparatus of the elephant. Of course the mahout went barefoot. Shoes would have hurt the elephant's trunk.

Elephants are not usually reared in captivity, but wild ones are caught and tamed. When a herd of the wild animals is caught in the enclosure made for this purpose, experienced mahouts on old and well trained elephants go in among the herd and capture the animals one by one and tie them to trees by the feet with chains.. After the first excitement of capture is over, two trusty elephants are taken one on each side of a new one. They stroke it with their trunks and seem to explain to it the new duties it is expected to perform. In a remarkably short time the new elephant understands the words of command as given by the mahout and it is driven about at will.

Intelligent as they are and trusty as they are, elephants are not always kind. While we were in India an account appeared in the dailies of two elephants that had been taken to bathe in the river near Benares. They became angry at each other. The drivers lost control of them entirely and they raced furiously through the streets of the city throwing things at each other with their trunks. The most convenient missiles they could find were men and they picked up one after the other and threw them back and forth as they rushed along. Several men were killed and many injured in this way before the furious animals could be brought under control.

The price of a good elephant is from five hundred to a thousand dollars. If an elephant is sold, his mahout usually goes with him, since he can care for the animal better than any stranger, and the elephant learns to love his keeper very much.

Elephants are not mentioned by name in the Bible. Some think that the Behemoth of the book of Job is the elephant, but this is not certain. The mention of ivory in connection with the splendor of Solomon indicates that elephants were know in his day and hunted for their large tusks; for, you know, ivory is usually obtained from the tusks of these huge animals.

While seeing the intelligence of the elephant, I often feel sorry that those who care for him, the people of India, do not as readily yield themselves to the control of Him who has done so much more for them— our Lord and Master, Jesus Christ.

CHAPTER 19

REFORMING AN INDIAN MISSIONARY'S KITCHEN

The trails of the missionary do not all come from the side of His work which has to do with dealing in a direct manner with the non-Christian people in regard to their souls.

In order to do effective work of any kind the missionary must live. The problems that come in connection with keeping the body and soul of the missionary together are numbers. While his first concern is in regard to spiritual things, and he has the promise that the necessary things of life will be added to him if he seeks first things first, eating and drinking and clothing must necessarily be so different from what he had been used to do that the proper amount of proper thought is due these proper physical needs.

Coming from a well-ordered American home the young missionary wife is considerably taken aback when she is told that she has no business in the kitchen. She has had dreams of how she was going to cook for her precious missionary husband and see to it that he has proper food at any

The Interior of a Missionary's Kitchen

rate, even if the climate is not all that might be desired to insure proper environments for good health.

She is apt to ask, "Why may I not cook at least part of the time?"

The older missionaries put her off as best they can and try to keep her out of the kitchen as long as they can.

But one day—at least this is the way it went with several that I know of, and one in particular—curiosity, faithfulness to duty, a sense of responsibility, and perhaps several other virtues and near-virtues get the better of her and, defying all orders and entreaties, she bodily presents herself at the kitchen door.

She does well if she goes no farther than the door.

The cook is in consternation, for the new mem-sahib does not know his language and his English is almost unintelligible to her as is his Hindi. How can he explain to her why it is that the meat that is to be cooked for dinner is lying in a dish exposed to flies and in the same dish are the unpared potatoes, the cabbage, and several other commodities usually kept separate in American homes? How can he explain to her that it is all right when she points to the pile of bones in the corner back of the door? When the cook's boy blows the fire with the bamboo pipe and the ashes fall all over the meat and the other contents of that dish, how is she to understand?

The new missionary sister comes in from her visit hot within and without—and with an indignation that she feels is very, very just.

How can the older missionaries tolerate such conditions? It isn't right!

A Great Purpose is forming within her.

That night before she falls asleep, she sheds a few tears, and thinks it all over. At last her Great Purpose is complete. She sighs, then calmly drops off to sleep and dreams of events for the morrow.

The morning finds her awake with the break of day.

She allows the early breakfast (choti haziri) to pass under the old order, but as soon as this meal is over she sallies forth to put in operation the New Rules.

It is needless to describe the process of cleaning. You can imagine what you yourself would want to do under the circumstances. After a

A Coolie Carrying Grain to the Market

couple of hours the new missionary sister smiles a smile such as only a clear conscience can prompt and says to the cook, "There! Isn't it better?"

She imagines that one sight of a kitchen so clean as that would inspire the cook with a desirer to have it thus always.

But alas!

The next day she visits the kitchen again.

Of course it will take weeks for the smoke to get as bad as it had been and some of the things she had put to rights are still in place, but for odd things to do and queer places for misplacing things, trust an Indian cook who so far loses his idea of his position to try to think. His business is to obey orders, not to think; for if he tries to think he is almost certain to think wrong—from the new missionary's stand point.

But whence this headache—this dizziness?

Too much exposure, too much tense exertion under the heat of the tropical sun. The protest of nerves and nature is imperative. The new missionary sister realizes that prudence is the better part of valor and withdraws her forces while she has any forces left to withdraw.

She resolves to visit the kitchen again as soon as she has rested up a bit. Other duties demand her time and she does not get back to the kitchen for a week. It would be cruel to describe that visit.

If our young missionary sister is wise she will have learned her lessen by this time and be satisfied if the results that come from the kitchen to the table are tolerable and will not be too punctilious about the process by which the tolerableness has been attained. She has learned in a sense that the great essential is not "meat and drink."

But why should the missionary tolerate a kitchen fifty feet away from the dining room with its little open "stoves" with smoke going out all around the little cooking pots? What's the use of all the servants? Why do not the missionaries do their own housework, just as they certainly would in America? Why not have an American stove and cook American ways? Why? Why? Why?

There is one word that answers every question—INDIA.

You are not in America when you are in India.

There are some who have tried to use the American ways in as nearly American kitchens as it was possible for them to have. To their credit and with deep respect to them it may be said that some of those who have tried these experiments have succeeded—at least in part. Many who have tried these ways have utterly and dismally failed. Some are paying the extreme penalty and their bodies rest in the long sleep beneath the tropic sun.

And even if success should reward the efforts—complete success—the question would still remain, Does it pay in the long run? Does it pay to send missionaries out all the way from America and support them in India at heavy expense to do the work that can be done at out-fourth the cost of persons accustomed to the climate and that can be influenced at the same time for good by the contact with the Christian spirit of the missionary? If the missionary is what he ought to be, the more people he comes in direct contact with the more he will influence for Christ.

With a reasonable amount of care, it is possible to have food prepared, even in India by Indian methods, in such a way as to be reasonably safe and sanitary. But if the missionary undertakes to be cook and table-boy and dish-washer and sweeper and ayah and messenger and gardener and milkmaid and all the other things that require a division of labor in India there are sure to be one or more unsatisfactory results.

There will be no time for language study.

There will be no time for Bible teaching.

The Indian people will feel that the white people are entering into competition with them in labor and will lose their respect for the missionaries.

The great work for which missionaries are sent to heathen lands will not be accomplished—witnessing for Christ.

The missionary, unaccustomed to the climate and its limitations, and unaccustomed to the ways of the country, is almost sure to break down in health under the pressure of manual work.

And now, if those lines should be read by some one who has an Indian missionary life in prospect, and still has a vague sense of desire to reform the Indian missionary's kitchen, let me give you one sentence of advice: Wait with your active reform, work along these lines until you have been in India for ten years. In that time you will have had time to gather a sense of the real difficulties and will be far more competent to offer the proper solution for the difficult problems than if you were to try to change things radically a month after you arrive in India.

CHAPTER 20

THE FIRE WORSHIPERS

When your ship leaves the port of New York, you step on board from a pier made of wooden piles driven deep into the ground and covered with framework and planks of wood. When you land in Bombay you step upon a structure of blue or gray granite firmly laid in cement. You pass the custom house after the usual routine and enter the city and are struck by the dignity and beauty of the buildings, the wide avenues, and the idea of solidity and permanence everywhere in evidence.

You ask in astonishment, "Where is the enterprise that prompts all this proof of stability?" And your informant replies by pointing to the man dressed in flowing robes and a shining, wedge-shaped head-dress and saying, "Men like that."

"Who is that?"

"That is a Parsee. The Parsees are the wealthiest and most highly educated class of India's people."

It was a Parsee that founded the Bombay dockyard in 1735 and the post of Master Builder has been filled by one of his descendants ever since.

The Parsi Tower of Silence

Surely you have heard of the Parsees. If you have heard nothing else about them you have heard of their peculiar method of disposing of the dead. They do not bury their dead as do the Christians and Mohammedans, for that would, they say, defile the sacred element of earth. They do not bury in the the sea, for that would defile the sacred elements of fire and air. It is these "elements"— earth, air, water and fire—together with the sun as the origin of fire, that the Parsees worship.

I do not know who originated the present plan of advising all the ways of defiling the elements, but the plan is most remarkable.

As you drive from the dock to your boarding house, you skirt the shore of Back Bay, around which a large part of the city of Bombay is built. Your eye catches a beautiful hill to the west, covered with palm trees and finely built mansions.

"Malabar Hill," says your informed companion. "On that hill live many of the wealthy Parsees, and on that hill the remains of their dead are exposed to become the food for vultures."

If you are like the writer you would be all interest at one and would be anxious to know more about these remarkable people.

In order to see the "Towers of Silence" in which the dead are exposed, it is necessary to obtain a permit from the secretary of the Parsee community whom we find in a large school for Parsees on Hornby Road. The secretary is very kind and polite and the permit costs us nothing. It states the name and occupation of the leader of the party of visitors and is unlimited in time. It is good until used.

Along a perfectly kept driveway we make our way to the entrance of the beautiful garden in which the towers are built. The city's storage reservoir for water is not far distant. Nature and man's art have combined to make the place as attractive as possible. Until you are actually within the place, there is not the slightest suggestion of the gruesome work done there.

Funerals are held at certain times of the day and at these times visitors are supposed to be excluded. But we were fortunate on one occasion to be allowed to see the funeral procession pass up the hill and into the gate. On another occasion we saw a procession return from the tower.

White-robed, consecrated corpse bearers take up the dead body and bear it to the place within the garden where the sacred dog is kept. He looked to us like a very ordinary dog, wholly unconscious of the place of great responsibility he is supposed to fill. He looked at us as any dog might look at strangers. Having had a hint, I asked the guide, "What is the business of the dog?" "The dog looks at the corpse as it is brought in." I questioned further but that was all the aged Parsee guide would tell. From other sources we learn that the look of the dog is supposed to drive away evil spirits from the soul of the deceased. If the dog refuses to look at the face of the corpse it is considered an evil omen, purporting ill for the destiny of the departed.

We were allowed to go within thirty yards of the Towers of Silence. None but the dead and the consecrated corpse bearers are allowed to go any nearer. On the top of the towers were the vultures sitting, waiting for their hideous feast.

Inside the building near the entrance of the garden, the guide showed us a model of the towers. There is a circular platform about thirty feet in diameter, sloping toward the center. There is a deep well in the center of the platform and from the bottom of the well there are four dains leading out to four other wells still deeper. On the platform around the well are three circles of niches for the reception of the dead bodies. The outer circle is for men, the next for women, and the inner circle is for children. A high wall surrounds the platform, with a small gate at one side, reached by stairs.

A Parsi funeral is always a "walking funeral." No matter how wealthy the man may have been, he is given a funeral on exactly the same basis as the poorest. The corpse is borne in front and the mourners follow—only men—in pairs, each pair holding a handkerchief between them. At the thirty-yard limit the procession halts, the sacred dog performs his part in the ceremony, and again the body is take by the corpse bearers and placed within the gate in its proper row on the platform. All clothing is removed and the corpse bearers hastily withdraw. The vultures on the wall around the tower pounce down and soon there is nothing left but bones. The bones are thrown into the well after a few days and disintegrate.

The Parsees were originally in Persia. From there they fled because of Mohammedan persecution, and came to India about the year 700 A.D. Having obtained permission from the Hindu Raja, they erected a fire temple and kindled their sacred fire at Sanjan, on the west coast of Gujarat in 721 A.D. From this place they have spread over the west coast of India and, for purposes of trade, to other parts of the world. Parsees number a few over a hundred thousand. They make no converts from other religions and so do not multiply rapidly. In fact they will not admit any into their society except those who are born of Parsee parents. It is also true that very few of them are converted to Christianity or other religious faiths. There have been a few notable exceptions, one with whom we were personally acquainted was M.H. Mody of Bombay. He is from one of the most prominent Parsee families. It was the Mody family that founded the Bombay towers of silence. One very old tower is pointed out which is reserved for members of the Mody family who die in the vicinity of Bombay. There are several other towers used by the general Parsee community.

M.H. Mody has suffered untold persecution because of his becoming a Christian. But he bears it all with true Christian fortitude and continues to witness for the Master in every way possible.

One feature very much to the credit of the Parsees is the elevated position given to women as compared with Hindus and Mohammedans. More than half the Parsee women are able to read and write and the proportion is rapidly increasing. Young women nowadays are generally educated in English as well as in the vernacular. Parsee ladies go out in public with their husbands and brothers or fathers as freely as European ladies do. Neither Hindus nor Mohammedans are permitted to do this.

Parsees are not idolators. They worship faithfully, according to their religious forms, the sun and the four "elements" before referred to. Their favorite plea of prayer is by the sea shore or on the bank of some stream. As they untie and tie again their sacred cord, they repeat prayers the meaning of which they do not in the least understand. As they mutter, they blink at the sun, they bow toward the water then to the earth, then toward the air over the earth, and they feel that somehow they have done their religious duty.

You may have seen the name spelled "Parsy." That is the spelling I prefer. The reason I have not used that spelling in this article is that I was afraid the readers would pronounce it "Pars-eye," and that would make an Indian ear tingle.

CHAPTER 21

HOW THE DHAMTARI LEPER ASYLUM WAS FOUNDED

On the outskirts of the village of Dhamtari, along the road leading to the Mahanadi river and beyond it to Sihawa, stands the famous temple of Balai Mata, much frequented by the Hindus of Dhamtari and vicinity.

Many years ago there came to the vicinity of this temple a group of persons afflicted by that dreadful disease, leprosy. They were from different villages and from different castes, but they were drawn together by common interest and by a common affliction. They built themselves rude huts and lived largely by begging. Wealthy men of Dhamtari annually gave sums of money to this leper community in order to make it less necessary for them to come to the town for the purpose of begging.

Another source of revenue for the lepers was the travelers who went by the road past their settlement. The traveler of supposed wealth and distinction often found a line in front of him as he came near the Bilai Mata temple. Before they opened up the line the lepers demanded a sum of money. The traveler dared not touch the lepers in order to force his way

The little chapel at the Dhamtari Leper Asylum that has served for man years as a shelter for the lepers as they attend worship. The end walls are built up, but the sides are open except for pillars to support the roof and vines which sometimes serve to keep out the sun. It is in bad repair and it is hoped that soon a better structure will replace it.

through, and the lepers stood their ground. It was little, if any, better than highway robbery, but no officer dared touch the lepers to punish them. This was the condition of things when the rains of 1899 failed and the famine of 1900 came on.

When the pinch of famine began to be felt, the lepers had a hard time of it. Begging was not so profitable as before, for many of the people who had been in the habit of helping them were now as poor as themselves. Famine kitchens were opened for the poor and helpless in various places but the lepers could not go to them for food. They could not go to the relief camps and work, for they were crippled by the disease. Besides, if they had been paid in money, who would have wanted to take their money?

In these circumstances, there came along the Indian Assistant Commissioner, Raghu Nath Rao by name, with a happy plan to make a separate kitchen for the lepers where they might be fed by themselves. His plan was approved by officers high up. The lepers were moved to a vacant space near a tank, temporary huts were constructed, and a regular famine kitchen was organized for the helpless ones. Thus things passed happily until the close of the famine in October, 1900. The begging ceased. Government paid the expenses of the up-keep of the leper kitchen and the leper community settled down to an enjoyment of conditions and they saw little reason for wishing to change for all time to come.

Raghu Nath was a master of English. He was also a master of explanation. His fellow officials with fairer skin than his nick-named him "The Plausible" because he had such a plausible excuse for everything that happened or did not happen. But in my memory he shines as a bright example of the highest type of non-Christian India. He seems to have a spark of genuine charity in his bosom that was well-nigh fanned into flame.

It was Raghu Nath Rao that suggested and urged the changing of the leper kitchen into a permanent leper asylum. He was seconded by Madhu Rao, also a famine officer of considerable merit. Captain McNabb was Deputy Commissioner in those days and he was one time discussing the future of the Dhamtari leper kitchen with one of the Raipur missionaries.

I remember how I resented the idea when I heard that he had said that he supposed that ultimately the leper kitchen would pass under the control of the Mennonite Mission. Had we not work enough and far more than we could do? Had we not already an orphanage with hundreds of children depending on us? Where was the strength to see after additional work? Where should the money come from to sustain such an investment? But that is how it came to pass nevertheless.

The famine kitchens had been closed, one by one. The last one to be closed was the central kitchen at Dhamtari. We supposed that the famine work was completed so far as our relationship with it was concerned.

But the next morning came to us the clerk of the leper kitchen with a question: What was to be done with the lepers? Should he issue to them their food as before or would the leper kitchen have to be closed as well as the others?

The lepers?

We had forgotten about them. We thought rapidly. Government orders were that when persons were dismissed from famine kitchens to their homes or villages, they should be given what was called "valedictory dole" of rice to last a month. By an easy interpretation of orders, the rule would apply to the lepers who were dismissed from government support, even if they did not move their living place. We had a supply of government rice on hand that was not salable and would not be available for any other purpose than famine relief, so we measured out a month's supply for the lepers.

And we purposely made a mistake in measurement. It really turned out to be enough for two months. The government officers were lenient and they did not hold us to a strict account for our mistake—in fact, they fully approved it.

C.A.P. Rogers, Assistant Commissioner and Famine Charge Officer, happened to know the address of John Jackson, then Organizing Secretary for India of the Mission to Lepers in India and the East. At his suggestion we wrote to the Organizing Secretary and in reply received a donation of fifty pounds Sterling ($250.00) for immediate needs of the Leper Asylum.

It would make this story too long to tell about the Committee of Dhamtari Gentlemen who at first were to control the Asylum, about how they got tired of the job before they began, how the Rs. 450 ($150.00) contributed by them was turned over to the Mennonite Mission, how the land for the Asylum was donated by the village owner of Dhamtari, how the 3 acres of land was sold to the Mission to Lepers in India and the East for a rupee (33 cents), how additional land was obtained for the use of the Asylum on the occasion of the visit of Thomas A. Bailey, who succeeded Mr. Jackson as Organizing Secretary, how prominent officials came and went and gave encouragement and advice and approval to the work, and how new buildings have been erected on new ground. The Asylum prospers and is one of the bright spots in our memory of India and one of the most pleasant places shown to visitors to the American Mennonite Mission.

Nearly all the inmates of the Asylum are Christians. No pressure is brought to bear upon them to make them become Christians when they enter the Asylum. Exactly the same treatment is given to all inmates, whether Christian or heathen. But the very atmosphere bears with it an influence for the divine Master and nearly all, sooner or later, embrace the Christian religion.

CHAPTER 22

AT THE
KORHI KHANA

What's the Korhi Khana?

Literally, it means the house for lepers. As the term is used in India it means the leper asylum, with its various houses, enclosures, gardens, and all that pertains to them.

It is Sunday afternoon. It is nearly four o'clock and the piece of railroad iron—or steel, rather—is being beaten as a signal for the lepers to assemble in the little building they call their "girja" or meeting house. Down through the mango grove comes the missionaries' tonga, and the steady "jing, jing, jhg" of the bells on the oxen announces to the lepers that the minister who is to preach to them that afternoon is coming.

The tonga stops outside the limits of the asylum and the missionaries dismount and go toward the little chapel. A beautiful garden has been planted between the walk and the chapel. Tall castor plants, with their beautiful notched leaves line the walk. Brilliant cock's combs, and an endless variety of other flowers are planted in neatly

The American Mennonite Mission's Book Depot in the bazaar of Dhamtari. The words, "Mission Book Depot," are seen on the sign, and the Hindi letters underneath spell exactly the same.

arranged beds all about the little space. To our right, near the men's quarters, is a grove of banana plants three time as tall as a man, with their rich clusters of fruit. A similar grove is straight before us within the women's compound.

As we enter the vine-clad chapel, with its cement floor and open sides, the lepers all stand up and give the universal Eastern greeting, "Salaam," with the hand raised respectfully to the forehead. It is a beautiful greeting. It means "Peace." This greeting is used in Palestine as well as in India and I cannot help believing that when our risen Lord greeted the disciples with "Peace be unto you," He utter this word.

The missionaries sit on chairs at one end of the building. The lepers sit on the floor in rows. One of the most pathetic memories of India is the song-voice of the lepers. The metallic tone is common to lepers all over the country. But they used their voices in genuine praise and prayer.

I shall never forget the earnest face of Alam, a leader among the men of asylum, as he sat on the floor in front. He drank in every word of the sermon, his keen eyes never leaving the face of the speaker, and the veins standing out upon his forehead in the intensity of his interest. That man could give a better statement of the essentials of the plan of salvation than many a church member in older Christian lands.

Another striking figure of the leper audience was the Mali, or gardener. It was he who was responsible for the beautiful flower garden, for the groves of bananas, and for the well-kept appearance of the whole place. He took a genuine delight in keeping the place clean and beautiful. He was a leper, far advanced in the disease, but with a true and faithful heart devoted to his Master and to the good of his fellow sufferers.

For a long time there was no one in the asylum who could read or write. At last a young woman who could read came to the asylum under pathetic circumstances. You undoubtedly know that children of lepers do not always contract the disease. If left with their parents to grow up, they generally do become leprous in time. Hence one of the prominent features of leper work is the care of "untainted children of lepers." By care and sanitation they frequently escape the dreadful plague.

Four such girls, sisters, came to the care of the mission and were placed in the room for the untainted girls. Indian children generally show a large degree of natural affection for their brothers and sisters, but these four sisters seemed rather more than usually attached to each other. One sad day the youngest of the four was burned to death while she was playing with fire. But it was even harder to bear when Rupotin, the second of the sisters, showed unmistakable signs of leprosy. All knew that she could not stay in the him for the untainted, but must go to the asylum to remain for the rest of her lifetime. She was willing to go, and even cheerful at the prospect, for she was an obedient child and never questioned the wisdom of the missionaries' decision. Soniya, the oldest of the sisters, with true sisterly affection, clung to Rupotin and begged that she might go with her to the asylum and care for her and protect her. She feared she might be lonely. Rupotin gathered her little belongings together, her school books, her song book, and her precious Bible, and with a loving "Salaam" to her many school-girl friends and her missionary care-takers, she left the mission home forever to dwell among the out-cast "without the camp." But she took the Lord Jesus with her, and daily read from His precious Word, both for her own comfort and for the edification of her afflicted sisters in the leper home. It was not many months until Soniya's wish to go to her sister was realized, for she, too, developed symptoms of the disease and had to leave the orphanage. Actual life in the leper asylum is not so bitter as it might seem to us who have such a thorough dread of the fearful malady. It would be hard indeed to find a similar number of people in India who are happier than this community of Christian lepers.

In connection with the work of the Methodist mission in Jabalpur, the largest city of the Central Provinces, there was a catechist, or Native preacher whose wife's name was Elizabeth. In course of time Elizabeth's husband died and Elizabeth worked along as a Bible woman in the employ of her mission. She read and sang well and was a very intelligent women. How she contracted the disease no one knows, but there was no mistaking the fact that she had become a leper, and it was not considered safe for her to be longer associated with persons from from the affliction.

Arrangement was made and Elizabeth found a home in the Dhamtari asylum. Her coming there was a boon both to her and many of the inmates of the asylum. She had some education and training in Christian work, and she found abundant opportunity for the exercise of her talents in teaching the leper women the "way of God more perfectly." Together they would read and study God's Word and sometimes the entire band would go out and sing for the villagers, who would stand and wonder that those who suffered such affliction could be so happy and be in possession of such a glorious faith.

Elizabeth has gone to her long home. Someday we hope to meet her again as she hoped when we said "Good-bye."

CHAPTER 23

HOME MAKING

Many days in our lives are important; yet, to most of us, the days of planning for and actually beginning homemaking are the most delightful and important of all. The Christian home is, perhaps, the most far-reaching in its influence for the good of all God's institutions.

One great task of the missionary in the East is to give to the home its real significance.

Oriental customs are widely different in most respects from those of the Occident. Not only does this apply to ordinary life and work, but to social customs as well. This would at least in part explain why Indian young men and women seem so much more self-conscious and bashful when in each other's presence than are the young people of their own country.

Marriages are usually arranged by parents or guardians and this custom gives the "papas" and "mamas" of large orphanages a heavy responsibility.

Hindi wedding. The bride and groom are seen to our left,
with their faces concealed by the curious matting of reeds and flowers.
The bride is to the right had of the groom.

"Papa" is seated in his office busy with the morning tasks. In comes an orphan boy, now grown to vigorous young manhood, with a very dignified and respectful "Salaam." He seems a bit ill at ease, and not nearly so hurried with his request as the orphans usually are when they have some trifling matter to bring before the missionary. The interested "papa" notices this, and leans back in his chair, ready to talk things over calmly and deliberately; for he sees that it is a bride and a home that the young man is interested in.

B has been observing, of course; and a little skillful questioning brings out the fact that D, a nice little girl in the orphanage has been elected as the sharer in the new home-to-be.

"Can you support a wife?" asks "papa."

"I think so," replies B.

"What can you do?" is then asked.

The boy replies a bit hesitatingly, yet confident that he has a work and that he can do it so that it will be a means of support. This young man, by the way, was a teacher in the blind school. He had a fair education. He was homely and awkward but patient and faithful—a plodder and not afraid of work. These observations, however, were quietly made without in the least suggesting them to the boy.

"Can you build your house?" then asked "papa."

"Oh, yes;" replied B, "I know how to build and I have saved up a bit of money for myself." He has been receiving a small allowance for his teaching.

"Very well; do you think you will be satisfied with D as your companion in the new home?"

"Who knows? But I hope so."

"Well, we should see about the matter," replies "papa" and the interview closes.

B goes about his work and feels a bit more anxious to do his work well than before. A new aim and purpose; something more to live for. This proves an inspiration to our dusky Indian children as well as others. Our B has an aim in life. He aspires to that which is noble. He has had great odds against him but he is quietly, persistently pressing on toward a noble Christian manhood.

The missionary in charge of the girl's orphanage is next consulted. Is D engaged? No. Will she make the kind of wife B needs? She is a good girl, quiet, friendly, though rather undemonstrative, but a good worker, as is generally known, for she has done house work for the missionaries. Do you think she will accept B as her husband? That is a matter for D to decide but I rather think she ought to.

The next step in proceedings is to place the matter before D. This may take place sometime later, as a fitting opportunity affords.

In as quiet a way as possible, so as not to attract attention to the other girls, D is called into the presence of the lady missionary. There is some preliminary conversation regarding D's former home and associates, her education in the orphanage, and there is an easy turn in the conversation to the subject of her prospects. Then the important question:

"D, do you think you could keep house and cook for one of the boys in the orphanage?"

D turns her shoulder toward the missionary, pulls her sari (dress) over her mouth and says shyly, "Kaun jane" (Who knows)?

"Kaun jane?" is such a universal answer that an Indian says it many a time without thinking. In effect it means simply, "I do not know," but it is an unheard of thing for an Indian to say anything so direct as that. There was one time in Calcutta a Christian wedding ceremony in progress. The all important question had been propounded to the bride. Either her "coach" had not properly instructed the young lady or else she forgot what to say, and she answered very bashfully, "Kaun jane!" A word of explanation helped the matter out and she rose to the occasion with a proper, "Ji, han" (Sir, yes!)

Now it happens that D's mind has been running on this very subject of late, and I am afraid if all the secret cobweb lines of communication were known to the missionaries, it would be known that D knew for sometime that B had already spoken to "Papa" and that he had asked to have her (D) as his bride. But D acts her part well. She is very much

A group of Christians on their wedding day. The contrast between the simple Christian ceremony and the extravagant, noisy, and demoralize Hindu wedding is seen in so commonplace a product as this picture in comparison with the picture of the Hindu marriage a few pages back.

shocked by the news that is gently broken to her, but before she goes back to her quarters, she gives her word to be the bride of B "in two or three years." But the missionary lady well knows that D would be a very much disappointed girl if the wedding were to be put off that many months.

There is yet another ordeal that has to be gone through before the engagement is considered final, and that is the meeting of the bride and groom. This "ceremonial" takes place always in the presence of one of the missionaries. They never meet in private before their wedding. They never speak together except on such an occasion as this.

D is in the room when B is called. One frightened glance, and D turns her back upon her intended husband and stands at the very farthest angle of the room. If the room were larger, she'd get farther away still. To face him under such circumstances would be the height of impropriety. But the situation is trying to poor B.

Missionary to B: "Speak to her."

B: "D, I have to come to ask you to be my wife."

No answer.

A glance at the missionary and assuring nod, then B tries again, "D, I love you and I wish you would speak to me and tell me if you will accept me."

A slight shrug is all that D deigns to answer.

Missionary to D: "Speak to him, D, he is waiting for an answer. Did you not say that you will accept him?"

D: "Kaun jane."

Missionary: "But, D, you surely remember that you have already promised and B is here now to hear from your own lips your promise. You must speak."

Interviews vary. One girl, after the preliminary shyness, turned boldly upon her suitor and asked, "If I marry you, will you beat me?" He made the proper promise. Many ask this question of the missionaries, but not all are bold enough to make this requirement in person.

In the case we have had in mind, D finally made the necessary promise and the interview ended with a genuine American handshake followed by an Indian "salaam." Two very happy individuals left the missionary's room by opposite doors.

After this preparations for a new family began to progress rapidly.

B began building his mud-walled house. In this he was assisted by the missionaries to some extent, and the whole cost of the house was as much as four American dollars. This expense was mostly for roof and the door. There is no window. Labor was furnished by B himself.

But love in a hut makes a home. Without it, a palace is nothing but dead material. And I believe that the two whose "courtship" we have briefly traced founded a true "home" even if they did not know the word as we know it. They are still living and loving in their Indian home. Children have come to bless their union, and their life is a witness to the saving grace of Jesus Christ.

This story is as nearly correct as the lapse of a dozen years enables us to remember it, though, for the reason that the originals might see and read the story, the initials of the names are not B and D.

CHAPTER 23

FROM BOMBAY TO ADEN

The touring season in India is from October to February, for that is the cool and pleasant time of the year. In the hot season no one remains in India except those whose homes are there and those whose duties demand their presence there. The rainy season, while not so oppressively hot as the latter portion of the dry season, is too warm and too humid to be considered pleasant.

English officers, missionaries, and business people whose work is in India and whose "home country" is in Europe or America, try to arrange their furloughs from India in such a way as to escape as many "hots" in India as possible.

In consequence of these circumstances one finds that a great many people, tourists, officers, missionaries and others, are traveling toward India from the beginning of September to the beginning of January, and that from February to June the tide of travel is away from India toward Europe.

A street scene in Bombay on a very ordinary occasion. How a driver gets his carrier in safety thru this mass is a marvel to a stranger.

Toward the end of the cool season of 1908 it became apparent to all of us that a longer stay in India would be dangerous if not fatal to my life companion, and I began at once to arrange for passage to America. Permission to leave India had been obtained from the home Board almost a year previous to this, at the time of the operation in the Miraj hospital. But we had still clung to India in hopes that by some means or other physical strength might return to our patient in the land of such great need. In this we were disappointed, yet we were deeply grateful that there was a sufficient degree of health to at least begin the journey homeward.

For various reasons the Italian line steamship R. Rubattino was chosen for the eastern end of the journey. The sailings of this line were only once a month. March, April and May sailings were booked full. June 15 was the first date available. So we booked by that line for the June sailing and bent every energy toward getting ready for the departure.

The rains broke at Bombay on the thirteenth of June—just two days before our ship sailed. The breaking of the monsoon rains is always an event of much interest in Bombay. For weeks before, the weather bureau of the Indian government has been reporting the progress of the head of the southwest winds that bring up the rains from the Indian Ocean. When the rains begin at Colombo, in the island of Ceylon, the news is telegraphed all over India, and the character of the first rains is often correctly taken to foretell the nature of the entire rainy season. About a week after the rains begin in Colombo they are due in Bombay, and a week later yet they are generally found to have reached Dhamtari.

Well do we remember the down-pour of a Bombay rain. The first showers are not much unlike any ordinary thunder showers in America. Then follow general rains that continue sometimes for days and days without interruption. One such downpour that we can never forget was one that we went through to see a noted specialist in order to get the final verdict that led to the operation at Miraj a week or two later. The streets were washed clean and a stream several inches deep was actually flowing along through the thoroughfares. No wonder the great doctor advised going to a place less humid than Bombay for such a trying ordeal as an operation.

But that was a year before we finally sailed. The rains of 1908 were normal as to time and fully up to the normal as to quantity.

Brethren J.N. Kaufman and P.A. Friesen had come to Bombay to see us off. After we were on the boar they went around to the pier-head where the ship had to pass through the dock gate into the open harbor. As we passed swiftly through the narrow water-way, Brother Kaufman called to us, "They say there is a cyclone two hundred miles out at sea—don't know which way it is going." I called back, "Perhaps we'll find out in a day or two." It was our last spoken message from India's soil—it almost makes me homesick to think that in all probability it was the last we shall ever hear. A few moments later we were out of speaking distance, and few moments longer and we were out of sight. I turned to the steward and asked in my best Italian, "Quando sara colazione pronto?" (When will breakfast be ready?) He had a better comprehension of foreign accents than my Chhattisgarhi friends of long ago and promptly answered, "Ora." (Now.)

Mamma did not care to eat. She wanted to rest. Baby Ruth and I ate a hearty meal. Then I sang Baby to sleep and I dropped into the nearest bunk. I slept a little while—perhaps two hours. Ruth awoke and demanded attention. I rose to give her what she needed. At about the same instance my breakfast rose. My head swam, and a minute later I fell back to my pillow. So Ruth was sea-sick. Mamma, who had been sick before she went on board, escaped the worst features of the sea-sickness, but you can imagine her suffering as she cared for herself and the sea-sick baby in her weakness with her husband helpless.

Why was all this thus?

I had managed somehow to see the pilot leave the ship. The coming aboard of the pilot and his leaving the ship are two events that always are of vast interest to travelers and I seldom missed them. After we had crossed the bar at the entrance of Bombay harbor, the little egg-shell of a boat came alongside. Our big ship rocked from side to side and it was with difficulty that even that old, experienced man of the sea could enter the boat. At last he was safe in the life-boat, the rope that towed it alongside was cast off, our engines began to move and the pilot waved "Good-by" to the officers on the bridge, and we saw the last tie to India, the pilot, rowed over the tossing waves to the pilot ship which was anchored near the course of the ships as they came and went.

The early monsoon winds are no gentle breezes—they are strong winds and sometimes violent storms. The wind was on our port bow. As landsmen say, it was a little to the left of straight ahead. The mountain waves were about at right angles with the wind. That meant that our ship had to climb up the side of each wave in the teeth of the wind and plunge down the other side. In performing this operation the ship rocked from side to side and endwise in a most disconcerting fashion.

And this sort of thing kept up incessantly for five days, until we had gotten out of the course of the monsoon and near the coast of Arabia.

But we didn't see any waves. We hardly heard them except as they struck the side of the ship and washed our porthole window with a prolonged swish. Sometime the port-hole was darkened by being entirely under the water.

Those waves often broke over the deck and all doors and ventilator had to be closed down tight in order to keep out the sea. Part of the time a small door was open the leeward side of the cabin. And that was all the ventilation there was for the second-class cabin with some forty-five persons in a space none too large for their accommodation.

Besides it was hot.

If one managed to get up and about long enough to put on dry clothing, it would not take five minutes to saturate the entire outfit with perspiration. Such sweating led to "prickly heat." Mamma escaped some of that, but Ruth and I were covered with it from head to foot. Other passengers suffered likewise. When we got though the storm and began to mingle with fellow passengers, we found that nearly all had "peeled off" their epidermis in that frightful experience.

Not only did the passengers suffer, but the few stewards, and all were in the same plight. Only the head steward of the second cabin and one of the second class passengers, a jolly and ruddy Irishman, escaped entirely. One other steward, with much holding on and a very pale face, managed to get about to do a little. But every move caused him evident agony.

Days of pain in sickness on land may seem longer than those five days did on the Arabian Sea, but most of us were ready to testify that never before had we gone though quite so much misery from physical distress as on those days of storm, but the darkest night has its dawning.

A few of the bolder spirits ventured out and came back joyfully testifying that there was hope. On the sixth day, closing my ears to all appeals, I went on deck, found and rigged up the deck-chair, and sat in it for about an hour. In the afternoon I took Ruth for while. There surely was hope of a better time.

The following day the whole family went on deck, and from that time on until we landed in New York most of our days and part of the nights were spent on deck, for we had delightful weather all the way.

Well do we remember the gratitude with which we greeted the sight of the Arabian coast and how we thanked God as we slowly swung into the harbor of Aden. The giant smoke-stack of our steamer was covered with salt from the spray of the ocean and the whole ship had a weather-beaten appearance. How gladly we welcomed the Aden pilot!

I was on deck as we arrived at "Steamer Point," Aden. On the bridge just above us were the officers, the pilot in charge, and the captain interpreting his orders to the Italian sailors. We could hear plainly the order given to "Starboard the helm," "Half speed," "Slow," "Stop." Then soon the order was given to "Drop anchor," and the message went to the engine room, to "Slow astern." The big vessel was quietly swinging at anchor in the clear waters of the Aden harbor.

And we meditated.

We were glad for the five days of suffering, now that they were over. Those days had been between us and the haven we so much desire. We were carried through them without our own exertion. Had our getting through depended upon us, we should have been helplessly lost. Those who had traveled the way before us and knew the way full well carried us through it all. When the time for rest came each minute order from the pilot was carried out promptly and to the very letter. Suppose when the order had come to the engineer to slow down and to stop, he had decided it was best to go ahead; suppose the caption had thought he'd rather pull port instead of starboard as they passed the shoal; suppose several others had decided they knew better than the caption or the pilot which way they should do or go—and we should soon have been as helpless as that wreck we saw in the harbor of Bombay as we came out or that tramp oil steamer we saw burning as we entered the harbor of Aden.

We can trust the Captain of our salvation to direct our lives. And it is just as important that we stop when He gives the signal for rest as that we go on when that is the order. Failure in the Christian life is invariably owing to failure to obey the Captain, for He knows the way. He has traveled the way before us and we can be assured that He will give no order but that which is for our good and for the good of the cause we hold dear.

CHAPTER 25

A COMPLETED LIFE– BIRAM

"Ham bhi ave?"

It was a quiet Sunday afternoon. The sun was sinking to a point where its rays seemed less fierce and we could venture out safely for a quiet walk for the purpose of collecting the shattered nerves of one who had suffered much from that bane of Indian mission life—nervous prostration.

Most of the children of the girls' orphanage at Sundarganj had gone out for a walk with Brother and Sister Lapp. A few of the smaller ones and two or three older ones who had not been so well remained behind. We had just started out when we heard the opening words, "Ham bhi ave?" (May we come too?) We looked to see the owner of the voice and saw Biram and a few others standing on the edge of the little tank that furnished the girls a bathing place in their compound.

The appeal was irresistible. We were not going far and these weaker ones could easily keep up with us, even if they might not be able to do so with the larger and stronger girls.

Grave of Jacob Burhard in the mango grove at Sundarganj, Dhamtari, who, after faithfully witnessing for the Master in India for six years, died September 29, 1906.

"Han, ana to!" (Yes, come along!)

How cheerfully they came. It was a great treat for them to come with us where they could receive a little measure of personal attention and not feel that they were only a few among so many that the missionaries could not notice them.

Biram was the one who had spoken. She was rather small for her age, but her mind seemed developed beyond her years. That was the first time she had impressed herself upon our notice. She had been "one of the orphans" up to this time, but from now on she was "Biram,"—a distinct personality.

Not long after this—perhaps a year or so— marriage arrangements were all the talk in the orphanages. Several of the boys had asked that they be allowed to "live for themselves" and that certain of the girls be allowed to share their houses with them.

Biram was one that had been asked for. Soon after that she came into the house to be our "house girl—the one that should make the beds, keep the living rooms in order, share in part the family life, help look after the baby, and, most important, receive from the "mem-sahib" as much inspiration as possible in the true secrets of home making.

Parsadi was the one who had asked for the hand of Biram. I suppose if it had been any boy in the orphanage that asked such a boon he would have been told that Biram was too young or he would have been put off on some pretext or other to cover the real reason—Biram was too precious a girl to be thrown away. I remember yet her cheerful "Ho, mamma" (Yes, mama), when she was asked to do some little favor. If being a favorite was a disadvantage, Biram was surely in danger.

But Parsadi—that was different. Parsadi was one of the tailer boys. His straight, dignified bearing and cheerful disposition were but a reflection of his character. He had been tested under trying circumstances and always seemed to ring true.

So on one glad day Parsadi and Biram were married. At the same time there were several other couples united in the sacred bonds, and they went out to live in homes of their own.

When our home was in Rudri Parsadi and his Biram lived near us—near us in more ways than one. They lived in two rooms that were the first to be build on the Rudri station—the rooms in which I lived alone in the rainy season of 1902, while the work on the other permanent buildings was being started.

In about a year, a little baby girl came to bless Parsadi's home. How welcome she was! How different was the reception of little Lina from that of many a little Indian girl. A Hindu father, when a boy is born and he is asked what has happened, says proudly, "A man has happened." But if the new arrival is a girl, he says with a mournful tone, "Nothing has happened."

We went to see the precious little baby frequently, but we could see all along that the mother was not well. Not long after the baby's arrival, Biram began to sink rapidly. Oh, how we longed to help our dear girl! Baby Lina seemed so well.

One night, when the baby was about two months old there came a call at the window of our sleeping room. I answered and Parsadi's voice said "Come quickly, Papa. I believe Biram is dying!"

When we got to the house we saw at a glance that his gravest fears were well founded. We remained with him until the precious young mother quietly passed over the river. A full, rounded out, Christian life completed.

Parsadi bore his affliction like a man and like a Christian. As he realized that his Biram was no more, while his strong body was shaken with sobs, he said pathetically, "She was so good! Never a cross word did she give me!"

Biram had early made the wise choice and had taken Jesus as her Savior. She lived her religion. "She was so good."

That afternoon, as we laid her body to rest, "Rakh, rakh men; dhul, dhul men; mitti, mitti men" (Ashes, in ashes; dust, in dust; earth, in earth), there were very few dry eyes about that grave. Her life was complete.

There were other bodies resting in that quiet burying ground, near the road from Rudri to the jungle, awaiting the trumpet call to meet the Redeemer; but our memories cling mostly about two mounds. One shelters all that remains to earth of a precious little baby boy, and the other covers the body of Biram.

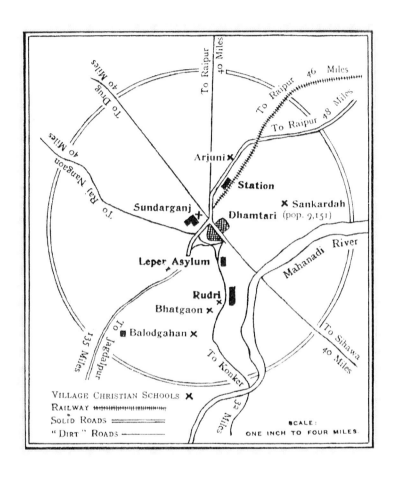

To Raipur 40 Miles

To Dhus 40 Miles

To Raipur 46 Miles

To Raipur 48 Miles

To Raj Nangaon 40 Miles

Arjuni ✗

Station

Sundarganj

✗ Sankardah

Dhamtari (pop. 9,151)

Mahanadi River

Leper Asylum

Rudri ✗

Bhatgaon ✗

■ Balodgahan ✗

To Jagdalpur 135 Miles

To Sihawa 40 Miles

To Konker 32 Miles

VILLAGE CHRISTIAN SCHOOLS ✗
RAILWAY ┉┉┉┉┉┉┉┉┉
SOLID ROADS ═══════
"DIRT" ROADS ────────

SCALE:
ONE INCH TO FOUR MILES.

Sketch Map of Vicinity of Dhamtari, India.